WHAT DONORS SAY
ABOUT CRISIS AID

Hand of Hope/ Joyce Meyer Ministries has partnered with Crisis Aid International since 2003. Our work together has moved from Afghanistan to Haiti, to East Africa. We value our relationship with Pat and his team and look forward to working with them for many more years to come.

DAVID MEYER
CEO, Hand of Hope, Joyce Meyer Ministries

Every major league pitcher strives to throw a perfect game. Pat Bradley and his Crisis Aid ministry throw one every day as they work to rescue people from hunger, sex trafficking, and life under horrible conditions. Born to Rescue features incredible stories about how God has transformed lives through Pat and his team. I highly recommend reading it because your life will be changed as well when you do.

– ADAM WAINWRIGHT
Pitcher, St Louis Cardinals

I know "Born For Rescue" will bless and challenge you the way it did me, plus make you shake your head a few times, seeing all the times Pat's life was spared in some of the world's darkest corners!!

– CHARLIE & JILL LEBLANC
Joyful Word Ministries

I'm an Ivy-educated white guy in America. An old white guy in his 70s, now; with millions socked away ~ NOT thanks to inheritance, I rush to add. We just didn't have kids. And we believed in saving. And, OK, my hobby was investing in emerging tech (it went pretty well).

This was all cultural retrofitting, though. I came from a blue-collar household. Thank you, mom and dad! My parents made sure my future could lead to a huge step up the socio-econ ladder (that Ivy university). And, later, in my late 50s I was content with the results. "OK, this is nice."

Then Crisis Aid opened a door I never suspected ... into a world of unimaginable suffering. That I could maybe do something about.

The bravery of Crisis Aid astonished me. They'd deliver aid to places where local military feared to tread. Even small contributions put in their hands made a decent difference. I fell in love with Crisis Aid. Then I met founders Susan and Pat personally, in Scotland of all places. I saw the pain, the determination and the hope in their eyes.

That's why I give. And give more.

– TOM AHERN

Tom Ahern … is one of the country's most sought-after creators of fund-raising messages." – The New York Times, Nov. 2016

"The reason I care about Crisis Aid is that I have witnessed the urgency first hand. My eyes have been opened to the desperation in which so many live. I have watched people on the brink of starvation be nursed back to life. Sadly, I have also seen some starve to death before my eyes. I have met many women who have been rescued from the horrors of the red light district, and then go on to live productive and godly lives. I have felt so honored to play a small part in saving lives and souls through Crisis Aid."

– FRANCIS CHAN
Author/ Speaker/Bible Teacher

We have been a part of supporting Crisis Aid led by Pat Bradley for several years now. Of all the mission projects we've been a part of over the years, Crisis Aid has been at the top of our list as an organization that really makes a difference in the lives of thousands of hurting people throughout the world! Our main investment has been in Ethiopia where we've built an orphanage, rescued human trafficking victims, fed the hungry, built medical facilities, etc. everything we've invested gets done and there is no missionary I have more confidence in than Pat Bradley!

– PASTOR DENNIS ROUSE
Founding Pastor Victory Church Atlanta, Author Speaker

"We had the privilege of getting to know Crisis Aid during a trip to East Africa a few years ago. We witnessed the incredible work God was doing through the Crisis Aid team meeting urgent physical and spiritual needs. From the red light district to the remote village, Crisis Aid was engaging people and quite literally saving their lives. We came home knowing that doing nothing was no longer an option. Gratefully, Crisis Aid generously worked with us to help us engage on a continuing basis with the beautiful people we had met on our trip. Through this opportunity our family has seen God grow our faith and thankfulness as we've seen Him provide through Crisis Aid beyond our wildest imagination. This journey with Crisis Aid has been nothing short of life-changing. Saying "yes" to the opportunity to come alongside Crisis Aid is the best decision we have made in our lives. Come join us!!"

– MICHAEL BLUE
President and General Counsel
Ron Blue Institute For Financial Planning

I became aware of Crisis Aid through a friend, and I'm grateful for his introduction. Pat Bradley and his team are changing the lives of people who are in desperate need. Through food distribution and their involvement with sex trafficking, Crisis Aid is making a difference. The stories from people whose lives have turned around, who have food to eat, or a place of refuge are heart-breaking but at the same time inspirational. I'm thankful to be a small part of Crisis Aid's support team, knowing that my donations directly help people who need help. Pat Bradley has a heart for people in need. He's a problem solver who sees poverty, hunger, and abuse as challenges to be solved. In Born For Rescue you'll discover not only Pat's heart, but you'll read about real people whose lives have been radically changed by Pat and his team at Crisis Aid International. As you turn the pages of Born For Rescue you'll discover how one person can affect change and you'll be challenged to allow God to bring to light His plan for you. I thoroughly enjoyed this book and highly recommend it.

— WAYNE HASTINGS
The Wayne Hastings Co, LLC

"What is the impact of one life changed forever? It is hard for us to comprehend the answer to that question in our limited human understanding. When I consider this, I recall Jesus' telling of the parables of the lost sheep, then the search for the lost coin, and finally rejoicing over the return of the prodigal son. If we have breath in us, it is quite likely we have experienced what it is like to be on both sides of these stories, and we are reminded of the goodness and grace of God. We are all people pilgrims in a land that is not really our home, and we are yearning to find purpose and meaning in our lives.

Crisis Aid is an opportunity to enter into the quest for the lost sheep, the frantic search for the lost coin, or the anxiety that comes from knowing your son or daughter has lost their way and you long for their return. I have had the honor and privilege of being connected to Crisis Aid for nearly twenty years now. For the first 18 years of that time, I knew in my mind what Crisis Aid was doing through the stories I read and pictures I saw, and I was grateful at some level, albeit easy to compartmentalize and return to the comforts of my day to day affairs.

In February of 2020, I had the opportunity to go to Ethiopia and experience first-hand the mission that Crisis Aid fulfills. When I looked into the eyes of the people, this indelible impression could no longer be compartmentalized. As we went to the remote places and saw families waiting for the kind of medical care for their children we take for granted, the poorest of the poor living in 80 square feet huts with no electricity or running water, and the dark streets lined with young girls in the red light district, I finally had an understanding of what breaks the heart of the Father. What I knew of Crisis Aid in my mind and had been able to 'forget about' at my convenience, now resides in my heart, and drives a passion in me that what I do has meaning - even if I have the easy part of just writing a check every now and then

While God does not need me to do what He is able to do, we are invited, through our connection to the life-saving mission of Crisis Aid, to impact the lives of lost and dying people whom God loves the very same way He loves us. Upon landing in the D.C. and boarding my two long flights back to the west coast, I cried uncontrollably the entire way home, realizing it was I who was lost." The story of God working in and through your life has me completely undone. For nearly 20 years I have had the privilege of having a small glimpse into your life's work and yet I failed to see how God was showing me His power at work in you.

— COREY DURBIN - CEO
Shared Health Alliance

I love Crisis Aid because it is one of the few Ministries that my wife and I have been invited to totally care for. Not just with our finances but also with my Spiritual gifts of teaching and Leadership for the extreme poor. I love that they are not just giving relief but also the cure which is the Gospel of Jesus. This has given me a sense of purpose and belonging with my brothers and sisters in Africa. I love that Crisis Aid does not just think of the present needs, but also of the long-term needs of the people that they serve. They look to each segment of Holistic ministry that they do as to helping it become sustainable. Incredible staff both in the US and overseas. I love working with all of them.

— DON CHRISTENSEN
Founder and Senior advisor,
Professional Athlete Division Ronald Blue Trust

Hope, gratitude, purpose, fulfillment, perseverance, sacrifice, courage, redemptive and eternal are words that I would use to characterize Crisis Aid International. Those words are powerful and something that I want to be a part of, not just as a financial donor, but as a human being. The work of Crisis Aid International is heroic and simply just good. This world needs more of the good, so I love being associated with an organization that is in existence solely to bring hope to people that are just trying to survive I have a deep admiration for Pat and Sue and the sacrifices they have made to help people around the globe that need help. I personally crave more of that in my life, and Crisis Aid International has created a gateway for me to participate in their mission, for which I am grateful. It brings me joy, but also an unsettled heart at times, because I want to do more! There's so much more that can be done, so I thank you Crisis Aid for your unwavering mission to change people's lives for good.

– LANCE KARNAN
Principal, Arc Wood & Timbers

Remarkable! What a testimony of a life lived for Christ. Pat's an everyday man, with a stained past – "for all have sinned and fall short of the glory of God" Romans 3:23. But, by grace, he has developed an extraordinary faith. He ministers to thousands of God's children that are in a life-threatening crisis. His appeal to you is to increasingly become more courageous in your work for Christ. Start with a small step – secure your first "yes" - gain confidence in the power of relinquishing to the Lord – then be amazed at what Christ can do through you.

Are you struggling to determine God's will for your life? Pat's desire in documenting his testimony is to encourage everyone to use their own Spiritual Gifts. "Having gifts that differ according to the grace give to us, let us use them." Romans 12:6 What is your calling? Possibly; service in your local community, teaching/discipleship, leading with grace, or acts of mercy and compassion to the elderly, sick or widowed. Pray this short prayer "make me know the way I should go, for to you I lift up my soul" Psalm 143:8b. If Christ is within you, don't settle for less than He demands – use your gifts. Pat's approach to provide relief in a crisis is to seek out the epicenter of the destruction – go where no one else is going to help. You can apply this concept in your local community - a crisis doesn't have to be monumental. Reach out to your neighbor who is experiencing hardship with empathy and kindness. Become someone who no longer accepts doing nothing as an option.

This is a call to action! Time is a wasting asset - you can never get back a wasted yesterday. There is no time like today. Like most of us, in Pat's deeply personal account of his life, he no doubt wasted days he wished he had back. But, by the grace of God, we would all admit his success is due to his deep faith in the unimaginable power of Christ to use an everyday sinner in building His kingdom. No matter where you are staring from, today make a decision and take a step forward. Christ will be with you all the way. You'll be amazed at what Christ can accomplish with a compassionate heart.

Pat's wife Sue played a significant role in the success of Crisis Aid, but the journey wasn't easy. After a broken marriage, she witnessed a transformation in Pat. But she also had to let go and surrender to the will of God. She realized that "God was doing things in His own plan that were higher than the plans I could have made for myself or my family. As I like to say, being in the center of God's will is the safest place to be. It is like the eye of the hurricane—a place of inexplicable peace as two-hundred-mile-per-hour winds swirl around you in every direction. Staying in that center is the key to not getting blown away by fear." They are two ordinary people, who by the grace of God, experienced His true redemptive power. It's available to all of us who place our faith in Christ.

If you have recently given your life to Christ, you may find yourself asking "What do I do now?" Maybe you've written a few checks to charity, been in the Word more often or spent a few hours in community service – but you realize "… faith apart from works is dead". James 2:26. Pat would encourage you to think bigger. Christ calls all of us to be disciples. Get off the sideline – you have a role to play – get in the game in a big way!

– TOM DEGNAN
Senior Vice President – Corporate Treasurer
Charter Communications

"Born For Rescue" by Pat Bradley is an emotional, exciting, encouraging and very human story of a man transformed by God to do what some may call "the impossible." But Pat kept saying yes, though at times reluctantly, and God led him on countless adventures to love and care for hurting people all over the world. From struggling with alcoholism and a difficult divorce to redemption and later, dealing with the Taliban in Afghanistan and caring for dying babies and trafficked women in Africa, Pat has seen it all and he has responded to it all by God's grace.

"Born For Rescue" is an inspiring book that reminds us that, with God, all things are truly possible... and God can use YOU to do impossible things! As Pat says, "...Life in Christ should be the greatest adventure imaginable!" "Born For Rescue," shares the great adventure of one man's life and helps to prepare you for your greatest adventure as you follow Christ!

— REV. DR. RANDY MAYFIELD
Pastor/Missionary/Musician

We have few examples of what a genuine life of faith looks like today. I have known Pat Bradley for about 10 years, been with him in the field, and believe he and his team at ICA are the real deal. "When Doing Nothing is No Longer an Option (or whatever you end up calling the book)" illustrates a real-life path to courageous faith for anyone curious enough or motivated enough to trust that God is Who he says he is - eager to use anyone willing to stand up and rebel against injustice. Bradley's story demonstrates, once again, that even after great failure, and regardless of geography or circumstance, God is inviting us to reject complacency and fear and embrace the unique life of adventure he holds out for each of us.

J. GREG SPENCER

Co-founder of The Paradigm Project and

Common Good Marketplace

We have known Pat for over 35 years, and have always admired and endeavored to emulate his heart for the hurting!

In the early days as a successful business man, he was always drawn to books about the suffering and persecuted church and needs around the world. We were so blessed to watch he and his wife in the early years take bold steps into international missions, and now into the amazingly fruitful labors of Crisis Aid around the world and at home.

We were also privileged to join them on a trip to East Africa, and experienced firsthand the gravity of reach that they have and how many lives are being sustained and improved because of their sacrifice. It is truly astounding what the Lord has done and continues doing through them!

Reading "Born For Rescue" made me ask better questions about my own life and ministry, as happens whenever I'm around these guys or read about their latest exploits. I see all they're doing to comfort the hurting and free the captives (literally AND figuratively), and this helps clarify and purify my own vision.

This book is filled with so many remarkable stories of how an ordinary guy is used to do extraordinary things. I almost wouldn't believe that they could be true except that I had the privilege of traveling with Pat and seeing some of these stories with my own eyes.

— BRIAN MOSLEY
President, RightNow Media

I know and trust Pat Bradley. He is the model of what phrases like, "refuse to do nothing ... do what you can ... take step one ... keep saying YES", really mean

— BOBB BIEHL
Author / Executive Mentor

"This book is more than a thrilling page turner. It's a true story of how one ordinary life who is committed to God and is willing to dare the impossible can make a difference in the world. You can too".

— PASTOR RICK SHELTON
Founding Pastor Life Church St. Louis, author and speaker

PAT BRADLEY
WITH JOHN DRIVER

BORN FOR RESCUE

FINDING PURPOSE
BY REFUSING
TO DO NOTHING

iDisciple® | **Publishing**

BORN FOR RESCUE

Published by iDisciple Publishing

2555 Northwinds Parkway, Alpharetta GA 30009

ISBN: 978-0-578-95655-8

DEDICATION

This book is dedicated to you, Susan.

Without your unwavering faith this book would not
exist. Your belief in the dream God gave us has never faded.
This dream has only grown over the years.
Your belief in God has become the foundation on
which helping millions of people rests and to
continue to help millions more.

Thank you for taking me back, because if you did
not there would have been no dream to believe in.

I love you forever.
I also dedicate this book to God,
thank you for everything you have
given and done for us.

FOREWORD

I will never forget the picture of the little girl up on the screen during a Professional Athlete conference I was speaking at a few years ago. She was from East Africa and looked like she was extremely malnourished with skin wrapped on some bones. She was about 5 years old and could not have weighed more than 20 pounds. The speaker that showed this picture was involved in this area of Africa. As the VP of the Professional Athlete division of our Firm, it is my role to the clients that I serve to look at for projects that they can get involved with. A month later I called the speaker who had showed the picture and asked him who the organization was that he was working in this area with these starving children. He said that it was a small ministry out of St. Louis called Crisis Aid International, and the founder was a man named Pat Bradley. I immediately contacted Pat. After hearing about what they were doing in East Africa with feeding the poor and rescuing Girls out of the red-light district of a big City, I decided to present a project to my clients and go with Pat and his wife to Africa.

I never realized what a change in my life this would be and the opportunities that would flow out of this ministry that was bringing so much bang for the dollars we were spending there. It has been my joy to work alongside of these humble servants for these past 5 years. I am honored to write this forward and encourage people to read it.

I usually do not read missionary biographical books of people that I do not know. I think this book you will find worth reading whether you know Pat or not. This book will captivate you and help you to understand how the Lord can use anybody He wants to no matter their background or their lack of expertise. Pat and Sue are great examples of people who answered the call out of the marketplace. We are all called to walk in the good works that He has created for us before the foundation of the world. What Crisis Aid has done is a testimony of how God uses small organizations to make a huge impact. You should not read these stories and think that you could never go or serve in tough areas of the world. Pat is not relaying these stories so that he can be the hero of them. He is trying to say that He is no more called than you or I are. You just need to do something.

I have spent many years on the Mission field like Pat. I can attest to the emotions that he expresses of fear in these sometimes-tight situations that we sometimes face out in third world countries. I want to encourage you to read this book as a challenge to see where God would have you join in. Remember

God has always been working around you and He just asks us to come join where He is already working, whether it physically going or sending with our financial support. It has been my joy to come work with this couple and ministry to help alleviate the pain of so many. The goal is always to bring the cure of the Gospel with the relief. I hope that you will see how the Lord has used them and rejoice in the changed lives that only the gospel of Jesus Christ can bring.

– DON CHRISTENSEN
Founder and Senior advisor,
Professional Athlete Division
Ronald Blue Trust

NOTE FROM
THE PUBLISHER

In September of 2019, a number of us from Giving Company were able to travel to East Africa with Pat Bradley to see the work of Crisis Aid International up close and personal. Through an interesting twist of events that only God could orchestrate, we had started to support Crisis Aid a few years earlier by donating proceeds from our publishing (iDisciple Publishing) and streaming businesses (Christian Cinema). We need to thank Francis Chan, Kevin Kim, and Crazy Love Ministries for the introduction to Pat and his team, along with Emma Lieblich, who was our first team member to travel with Crisis Aid prior to our trip in the fall of 2019.

What we saw in Africa was the combination of poverty and neglect, met with care, service, hope, and redemption that would take your breath away. Pat allowed us to attend a graduation ceremony of girls who were trapped in a life of sexual slavery with no way out. Instead of being violated and damaged, they were now smiling and laughing with friends in their caps and gowns. They had been rescued. We saw a medical clinic caring for babies suffering from starvation and malnutrition. Pat would take the time to pray with parents and grandparents as these tiny children were admitted for medical treatment. The reception area and the entire courtyard were filled with people patiently waiting to receive care. We participated in food distribution, observed vocational training, and visited an orphanage for kids whose parents had died from AIDS. They had been rescued.

The reality is, we are all born for rescue. Some of us need rescuing from starvation and neglect. Others need rescuing from pride, selfishness, indifference, addiction, or whatever else may prevent us from serving God and others to our fullest ability. This need for rescue is what binds all of us around the world as products of God's creation. Pat has his own story of needing rescue, which you will encounter in these pages. But Pat then turned his rescue into action. He and Sue founded Crisis Aid International when they distributed rice in Sudan over 20 years ago. Since then, they have served over 3 million people around the world—providing food, medical care, jobs, education and training, and rescue from trafficking. Pat possesses a personal humility with a fire to make a difference unlike anyone I have ever seen. I hope Pat and Sue's personal story, along with the stories of the work of Crisis Aid, will propel you to embrace the rescue you need and the rescue you can deliver. Pat will be the first to tell you that your life matters, and you can make a difference in the lives of others.

It has been our privilege at Giving Company and iDisciple Publishing not simply to publish these stories in *Born for Rescue,* but to become a partner in Crisis Aid's journey of meeting the needs of some of the world's most vulnerable. It is my sincere hope and prayer that you will be touched and motivated by the words you encounter here.

DAVID

– DAVID HENRIKSEN
President and CEO
Giving Company/iDisciple Publishing

CONTENTS

ONE

DOING NOTHING

"Stop where you are!"

I didn't speak Pashtun, but I didn't have to wait for the translator on this one. I also didn't actually say yes, but stopping in my tracks was basically the same thing. *We're dead*, I thought to myself in English, along with a few other choice words. The man speaking to us was wielding an AK-47, as were the other six guys with him. I had gone too far this time. People often ask me what emotions I feel in moments like these. You may not like the answer.

I was scared sh**less.

Most people don't think of food delivery as a very dangerous job. Then again, most people probably haven't driven a truckload of food to Afghan refugees in a Taliban-run camp—a camp that even the UN itself is afraid to enter. I never dreamed that I would be doing such a crazy thing either.

You see, I'm just a guy in advertising.

It had been only eight weeks since the horrific attacks of September 11, 2001, and through a series of unpredictable events, the kind of events it will be hard to do justice to as I describe them in the pages ahead, I found myself in Pakistan riding in a truck loaded down with several tons of food. We were trying to deliver it across what felt like a war zone to get to a crude encampment—a refugee camp—of more than 50,000 starving people just across the border from Afghanistan. These people were fleeing the shock and awe of devastation still being inflicted by thousands upon thousands of American bombs falling across their homeland.

When I say it felt like a war zone, I mean that literally.

I guess I had it coming—this was the only time my wife and children had ever been mad at me for going on one of my trips abroad. Russia. Sudan. Ethiopia. Many others I will soon describe. My family somewhat understood the level of danger I might encounter, though this was not the only time I would find myself standing before soldiers, warlords, or AK-47s precariously pointed in my direction. My family usually didn't know, mainly because I've not always been real keen on telling them the whole story. (My wife, Susan, has actually learned quite a bit from the writing of this book.)

We had watched together in horror as the World Trade Center was struck by two hijacked commercial airliners. As the first tower crumbled under the extreme heat of the jet-fueled explosion and was about halfway down, I dazedly said, "Now I know why God told me to go to Afghanistan." Susan looked at me with the strangest expression of "have you lost your ever-loving mind?!" Honestly, I was surprised I had said it out loud, because I didn't mean to. That's another story for later, but it suffices to say that earlier that spring, I had sensed that I would be going to Afghanistan. I just didn't know why.

Until now.

Obviously, Americans were not allowed to fly into Afghanistan because of the war that was raging there. Pakistan would have to do. As was often the case, I really wasn't sure where I was going when I landed. I just knew I should go, so I did. Our rule of thumb has always been to seek out the epicenter of the destruction—where no one else is going to help—and to go there as quickly as possible.

My only contact for this trip was a Pakistani official named Shahbaz, a dear friend and a huge part of our story. He knew I was there and had passed along one or two contacts, including that of a translator, but other than him and my family, no one had any real clue about our actual location, which meant that no one would know where to look for us if something went south.

If there was a metaphorical border for things "going South," we were about to be literally detained at gunpoint there.

We had secured the truck and loaded up the supplies before meandering our way through a maze of narrow alleyways and streets crowded with thousands of people walking in every direction. We were already nervous being in this unnamed border town. Suddenly, a Jeep-like vehicle had appeared out of nowhere, blocking our passage on the extremely narrow road. The guys carrying the AK-47s looked just like characters from a TV show—fighting-age men in simple, dusty tunics and turbans. They sported short, black beards. Their faces seemed to be etched in stone with a collective expression of silent suspicion. Maybe I had heard wrong. Maybe God had not really sent us to this seemingly God-forsaken place.

Sure enough, they were Taliban—and they had us surrounded. As the translator spoke with the leader of the armed group, I waited for the worst. But to my surprise, gunshots never rang out and no one ever put a black bag over my head to whisk me away to some undisclosed location for ransom or execution. Instead, the translator approached me and said, "They are the bodyguards for the leader who runs the refugee camp. They're here to escort us there."

To this day, I'm not sure how they knew we were coming, but somehow they had been made aware of our mission to bring aid. The truth is, without their escort, we would have never made it to the camp alive.

The refugee camp was situated near the border of Pakistan and Afghanistan. It was winter, which meant that at night it was getting very, very cold—the windchill often reaching temperatures of twenty or thirty degrees below zero. People were still streaming into the camp by the thousands every day, escaping over the mountains from their recently leveled towns and villages with all the worldly possessions they could carry in their arms on a nightmarish journey lit only by moonlight and explosions.

Men. Women. Children. Babies. The elderly. Families. These were real people on the verge of freezing and starving because the leaders of the camp had nothing to offer them except what few supplies the UN was willing to drop several miles away from the camp. For the most part, all they could do to help these newly arriving refugees was dig holes in the ground so they could get out of the wind at nighttime—and a growing number of thousands upon thousands of people were just being left there to survive on their own. The world was doing nothing to help them.

Begin with Love

Pause.

You need to know a few things before we go any further, especially after reading a story like this one. You might be thinking, *This is going to be a book about some superhuman globe-trotter, and when it's all said and done, I will be inspired to give money. Ultimately, I'll be reminded that some people are super-human, but not normal people like me.*

Yeah, I'm not *that* kind of guy. I am a regular person, and I feel very unqualified to experience any of the things that have happened. Keep reading and you'll know why. For now, just know that I never went to seminary. I don't read ancient Greek. When I step on water, I sink. I get enraged. I become discouraged. I have failed. Sometimes I curse. I often make lofty promises that have no chance of being fulfilled unless something extraordinary happens outside of my control. When you read about my most important relationship in life and how I failed, you will gladly scrap any rose-colored illusions about my life once and for all.

LOVING THE "LEAST OF THESE" IS ONE OF THE PRIMARY WAYS I LOVE HIM.

It also makes sense, then, that I am *not* your typical author. The truth is, taking the time to write this book was something I did not really want to do. It's not that the stories are boring or not worth telling—they most assuredly are. The people you are about to meet in these pages are more precious to me than you can ever imagine. For some, this is my chance to memorialize them—to tell the story they are no longer here to tell. But I would much rather be out there living these stories than talking or writing about them—or writing about myself at all.

None of this is what I signed up for.

I never expected that desperate parents—people in parts of the planet so remote that even most of the citizens in their own countries never venture there—would put their dying babies into my hands. Cradling a suffering baby who is wasting away from starvation and easily preventable diseases was never what I thought I would do with this life—and knowing that these despairing families are expecting me to actually *do something about it* does not fill me with confidence or trigger some self-reliant, white savior complex. No, I feel their panic. I share their pain.

And I think to myself, *What am I doing?*

I've seen some incredible things, but I've also spent a lot of time shaking—both in my boots and with my fists toward the heavens. Many, many times, I've set out on operations that required millions of dollars to pull off with no idea where the money would come from. I've lost dear friends to persecution and unspeakable violence—champions whose courage was boundless and who dared to stand up for something they knew would land them between sinister enemy crosshairs. I've wept uncontrollably.

I've also experienced a level of joy I never thought humanly possible. I never thought that I would walk many precious young women down the aisle to meet their husbands at an altar of sacred matrimony—girls who, only a few years before, had been hopelessly trapped as sex slaves in vast, seemingly never-ending red-light districts stretching so far that it boggles and shadows the mind. I never knew how the appearance of a child on the verge of starvation could drastically improve in a few short weeks on a diet that includes eggs and milk.

How did it happen? God transformed my life and put within me a love for people that I never thought possible. This deep love has been the guiding force for everything that has happened. People have seen this love within me and sensed that it was placed there by Someone besides me. It's been pointed out to me by many people on trips, by doctors and nurses helping us save lives, and even by Afghan warlords. These stories have been written on the foundation of love—a love that I don't deserve and that I never thought was possible, yet it has produced impossible stories of hope and redemption in me and in others.

I began loving people that I had not even seen before—people that society often overlooks. The hungry. The slave. The homeless. The sick. It's all too easy to walk by them, not knowing how to help—or perhaps it's all too easy to forget that I have been in various levels of need myself. But Christ graciously reminds me that "whatever you did for one of the least of these brothers and sisters of mine, you did for me" (Matthew 25:40, NIV). Loving the "least of these" is one of the primary ways I love Him.

Though I felt this divine love within me and around me, I never knew how broken and enraged my heart could become until I experienced being a few days too late to provide a precious child what he needed to survive and recover. I've been stunned and perplexed that a mother could be willing to sell her own two young children to a brothel where they would live as sex slaves. I've felt these difficult emotions. But sometimes the most incredible light has emerged from the darkest moments. In fact, the death of one little girl in particular launched us into an entirely new way of thinking and working in East African villages and the surrounding areas. I also never knew how much one little girl, Zorha, could impact my life and the lives of thousands of others.

THIS LIFE IN CHRIST SHOULD BE THE GREATEST ADVENTURE IMAGINABLE!

Unfortunately, these are the kinds of stories that most people don't hear in church on a regular basis. Speaking of church, there is a good chance that if you're reading this book, you are part of a church. This is a wonderful thing. Unfortunately, though, many people in church sit week after week in boredom. They are bored with their Christian lives, so they stop asking God to include them in His great adventure of redeeming the world. They begin to believe that following Christ is a life of dull living, rigid rules, and weekly church attendance.

It is not!

This life in Christ should be the greatest adventure imaginable! What if I told you that God wants to do more in your life than you've ever envisioned in your wildest dreams? Does that sound too cliché or extreme? If so, then we're missing the adventurous truth of Scripture:

Now all glory to God, who is able, through his mighty power at work within us, to accomplish infinitely more than we might ask or think. (EPHESIANS 3:20)

Dreams really do come true, but some Christians have stopped dreaming on God's level. They forget that they are literally "God's handiwork, created in Christ Jesus to do good works, which God prepared in advance for us to do" (Ephesians 2:10, NIV).

We are often guilty of asking the Father for too little, and as a result, we experience too little of the work He is doing in the world. Along the way, we sit in the pews and do nothing, which becomes a crime against humanity by the ones whom God put here to serve humanity. None of us usually intend any harm; we simply stop dreaming that we might have a role in affecting eternity—not realizing that doing nothing is affecting the eternal cause, just not in the way God desires. We think that the radical stories of adventure and transformation are reserved for a special few and not for the everyday "normal" believer. We're missing the adventure because the Christian life has become a misadventure of boring pew dwelling.

Like you, I know all too well what it's like to read or hear stories from people in "ministry" and feel both the compelling need to put them on a pedestal and also the depressing need to remind myself that I'm *not* on that pedestal with them. I really do believe that I was born to do the things that I am doing, but I also know what it feels like to wonder if I'm qualified. As my family and our team will tell you, I have a very positive outlook on life and enjoy every day that I get to live. Even so, I also know what it's like to wonder if I'm not good enough. Not fully knowing how God really feels about you and about your life can make you feel this way. I once deeply identified with scarcity and insecurity. But God changed all that for me—and he wants to do the same for you.

DREAMS REALLY DO COME TRUE, BUT SOME CHRISTIANS HAVE STOPPED DREAMING ON GOD'S LEVEL.

Some well-meaning people have called me the Indiana Jones of missions. I hate that comparison, though I love those who have made it. Yes, there is some element of adventure to what we do, but we are not heroes who always emerge unscathed just before the credits roll. We deserve no credit. We have made many mistakes, lost many friends, and failed many times. Honestly, often I have been shocked that I returned home in one piece, as you will see. Our organization, Crisis Aid, actually started because of an argument I had with God on the border of Afghanistan and Pakistan—not exactly the most noble of beginnings. It's time for us to stop being surprised at brokenness and instead embrace its universal role in each of our lives.

IT'S TIME FOR US TO STOP BEING SURPRISED AT BROKENNESS AND INSTEAD EMBRACE ITS UNIVERSAL ROLE IN EACH OF OUR LIVES.

It is human nature to want to elevate other humans. We love the superhero stories and any narrative that makes a certain person seem better than the rest of us. Such stories infuse us with hope to keep reaching for where they are, but also make us feel shame that we never seem to get there. The truth is, they probably haven't actually "gotten there" either. Moving videos and photos of good, even incredible experiences usually edit out the unseemly parts. The moment you lost your cool. The moment you doubted God. The moment you wanted to burn it all to the ground.

I want you to see these parts of our story.

What happens when someone lesser than the rest of us—yours truly—experiences extraordinary things beyond his ability or expectation? I hope that it will ignite at least a tiny flicker within you to realize that you need not be extraordinary for God to do extraordinary things in your soul and in His world. "Normal" people are not only welcome; they are the key to God's whole plan.

What about you? What about recovering addicts? What about divorcées who work minimum wage jobs and struggle to make ends meet? What about parents just trying to keep their children from screwing up their lives? What about pew sitters with pacemakers and hotheads who are far from peacemakers? Where do they fit in God's big story of redemption and adventure?

In God's real story, you are on every page.

To this day, I still struggle with feeling like I don't belong here, wherever here may be. My bet is that I'm not the only one. I used to struggle with seeing others in ministry and wondering what it felt like to be in their shoes because I was convinced that there was no way what they were feeling was the same as what I feel. This is a common problem for Christians, but God had different plans for me, which included getting me out of my own head and into the middle of situations far, far beyond my qualification or ability. Otherwise I would have remained as

"NORMAL" PEOPLE ARE NOT ONLY WELCOME; THEY ARE THE KEY TO GOD'S WHOLE PLAN.

so many Christians live: somewhat aware of the vast needs in a huge world, sometimes feeling bad about it, but mostly doing nothing about it.

Forget Indiana Jones. Forget the craziness of it all. Forget whether or not your stories will ever look like mine or anyone else's. Forget trying to figure out what someone else who does things you don't do—or seemingly can't do—must feel like. For a moment, forget feelings altogether. When we forget these things, we can free up the necessary real estate in our minds that will allow God to simplify the whole matter in a way that goes far beyond mere good intentions or bad feelings.

For me, it all began when God showed me how He feels about the concept of doing nothing.

Looking Back Over My Shoulder

I first began traveling in the late 1980s with the purpose of serving the persecuted church around the world. There are some stories about these travels that I will share later, but for now, let's just say that I was still working in marketing and advertising and would use my vacation time to go to other countries to smuggle Bibles and other Christian contraband across their borders. I would also spend time with the underground churches and people who were facing persecution.

Things began to change for me around the year 2000. By this time, I served on the board for International Christian

Concern (ICC), an incredible organization that serves persecuted Christians around the world.[1] We began receiving what we considered credible reports about what was happening in southern Sudan and the atrocities of a civil war raging there. We decided to take a fact-finding trip to see for ourselves what God might be calling us to do there.

We flew from Washington, D.C., to Kampala, Uganda. From there, we drove about fourteen hours to the Sudanese border. The car must have been more than 110 degrees—unbearably hot, even with the windows rolled down. But things got worse as soon as we crossed the border. The conditions of the roads immediately deteriorated, so much so that it took us about three and a half more hours to reach the military checkpoint that was only five miles across the border. Four hours to go five miles.

That was my introduction to Sudan: nothing here was easy.

Over the next two weeks, we began meeting with local government, religious, and military leaders to hear their stories about the unfathomable terrors occurring all around them. The northern government regime known as the Government of Sudan (GOS) had been relentlessly attacking villages in the south. In addition to their own army, they were also funding various militia groups to carry out similar attacks.

They were opposed by the Sudanese People's Liberation Army (SPLA), but in most cases the GOS was attacking, looting, and destroying villages where there was no SPLA presence.

---

[1] Learn more about ICC and ways you can support their important work at persecution.org.

In other words, this was not just a war between soldiers—this was ethnic cleansing targeting civilians. They had already killed an undetermined number of unarmed villagers, often with the help of artillery, bombs, and helicopter gunships.

Their modus operandi was to attack these villages at night, rape and kill the women, kill the men, and sometimes take the children captive to be sold into slavery. At times, they would just wipe out the entire village with an unimaginable ruthlessness devoid of basic decency or humanity. The stories we heard disturbed me to my very core in ways I never thought possible. We crisscrossed South Sudan, moving in and out of active war zones and hearing chilling firsthand accounts.

Our primary objective was to evaluate the conditions that the survivors were living in so we could formulate a plan to help. After canvassing the area for two weeks, we couldn't even call their situation one of mass poverty because the term "poverty" wouldn't do it justice.

On our last day in the country, we came upon a group of about seventy men, women, and children. Their village had been attacked the night before, and they were the only survivors. There were numerous elderly people among them who were in bad shape. Many of the villagers' clothes were torn and ripped from running through the jungle bush—and their bodies were cut up, bleeding, and injured.

It was about 120 degrees that day, and this group of survivors huddled together under the fleeting shade of a small copse of trees. The shade stretched no wider than several hundred square feet, and they crammed together in it, just trying to find some relief from the blistering heat. Emotionally, they were reeling from the devastation. They had lost loved ones. Children. Husbands. Fathers. Wives. Mothers.

I put myself in their shoes—and I was never the same.

These people were hundreds of miles from food, water, and shelter, and we had absolutely nothing to give them. It was really an accident that we had come across them in the first place. I have never felt so helpless. Even if we could have walked to get water for them, they didn't have any cans or containers to store it. No plates or cups. No clothes. No blankets. No phones. Nothing. No one knew they were there. No one was coming to help. They were literally standing in the middle of nowhere, still looking back over their shoulders in case their attackers might emerge again at any moment.

And we had to leave them in this state of being—we had to go.

What happened next is something I remember like it was yesterday. We got into our car, and I was sitting in the back seat on the passenger side. As we started to pull away, and they were looking back over their shoulders in fear, I looked back at them over my shoulder, in turmoil.

A strong, undeniable thought entered my mind: *doing nothing is no longer an option.*

Instantaneously, I knew exactly what this meant. I knew that my life was about to change. Up to this point, I had my business and family life, and then my ministry life that I engaged in during vacations. But this was the beginning of God speaking to my heart and saying that He was changing the focus of our ministry from the persecuted church to the imminent, felt needs of people in serious trouble. I knew that this meant providing food, water, shelter, medical care, and whatever else was needed to forgotten people huddling in completely unseen places around the world with no hope of anyone coming to their aid. God saw them, and now He had allowed me to see them too—and everything had changed.

GOD SAW THEM, AND NOW HE HAD ALLOWED ME TO SEE THEM TOO— AND EVERYTHING HAD CHANGED.

This was a traumatic exposure for me, though it was nothing compared to the trauma those poor people had experienced. I was completely overwhelmed with what I had seen and heard. I was so angry that people could do this kind of thing to other people. I also had thoughts swirling in my mind of all the things that had to be done to begin organizing a plan to provide relief and aid to these places of greatest need.

I shut down. My mind, emotions, and entire being were so assaulted that I became unable to do anything else for a while.

In fact, after I got home, I didn't speak for almost two weeks—not to my wife, my children, or the people who worked for me at the ad agency. Everyone thought I had lost my mind. No one knew what was going on—I didn't even quite understand what was going on. Looking back, I think I was just processing everything I had seen. I had never before seen dead people. I'd never heard about babies being slammed up against trees, and now I had listened to the stories firsthand from mothers who had witnessed it happen to their own children. I had never seen children with their limbs blown off from bombs.

It was so much—and now maybe you understand why I haven't always been keen on talking about every thing I have seen. Regardless, God flipped a switch in me, and though I was completely overwhelmed by the thought of what I should do next, I knew beyond a shadow of a doubt that doing nothing was no longer an option.

I KNEW BEYOND A SHADOW OF A DOUBT THAT DOING NOTHING WAS NO LONGER AN OPTION.

Surrounded

Maybe these kinds of stories make you uncomfortable. This is not the kind of reading that will help you unwind after a stressful day at work. I get it. Maybe these kinds of stories make you feel like we did in the beginning of this chapter: surrounded by foreign, scary elements. Maybe you feel threatened, insecure, overwhelmed, or overstimulated by the negative realities of it all.

Let me remind and encourage you here at the outset of our journey: what I first feared and wanted to run from was not there to hurt me, but rather to protect me as I was escorted to places I could never have gone on my own to do work that I could never fathom doing under my own strength.

God has you surrounded, but He is not your enemy. This is not to say that He is safe or will only lead you to safe places or endeavors, but He is indeed trustworthy. And I want to show you how He has proven this to be true over and over again. The best way to show you is to transport you to some of the places we have been and to reveal some of the things we have seen. I want to introduce you to the people who have changed my life—and who, by God's grace, we have been able to help change as well.

When I thumb through my passport, each stamp inside is a reminder—a snapshot of the memories of that trip. Treat this book like the pages of a passport. There is no way I will be able to exhaustively share everything that has happened over the past forty years, but I can offer glimpses into what happened here and there—like stamps on the passport pages. My goal is to show you vignettes of different places and experiences, taking you with me to places you may have never visited before to see things you never knew existed. I want to share experiences and miracles that have taken place in the lives of those whom we serve.

This will not be a chronological journey, as you have probably already ascertained. The time line matters in places, but mostly we will jump around the world geographically throughout various years for the purpose of introducing you to the most memorable people and places we have encountered. To protect the dignity and privacy of our friends, I will often not use their real names, but their stories are absolutely true to the best of my recollection. I will also often use vague geographical terms due to politically sensitive situations still ongoing in some areas where we serve.

In many cases, these stories have been documented for the past two decades in our Crisis Aid newsletters and year-end reports . . . I'm pretty glad we took the time to create those now! To that end, I will also show you images of some of these unforgettable people and places in the photo section of this book. I wish you could see the thousands upon thousands of pictures we have accumulated from almost every place and project we have engaged, but there are simply too many to include. You can always visit crisisaid.org for more chronicled resources and to find ways to help continue the work.

I want to tell stories for people who can't speak for themselves, raising awareness and resources for those in greatest need. I want to help you see that I'm no different than you are, and that if God can use me, trust me, He can use you. If you will begin to believe that doing nothing is no longer an option, God will meet you there. Most importantly, I want these stories to glorify God—to elevate and magnify His message of hope, healing, and compassion.

There will be two times in the book, once near the beginning and once near the end, where my wife, Susan, will add some reflections of her own. She is my wife, best friend, and partner in every way imaginable, and the journey we have walked together is a wild one. To that end, we must leave the confines of Africa and the Middle East and dial this story way back to the late 1970s and early 1980s.

I told you that my trip to Afghanistan was the only time my wife became angry with me for going somewhere to help others. However, it was not at all the first time she had been angry with me for going somewhere to help myself.

Six years into our marriage, we had two beautiful children, Rebecca and Shawn. But things were not okay. One day Susan called me at work.

"Are you coming home soon?"

"No, I'm going out with the guys again. I'll be home later tonight." Partying with my friends had become a nightly ritual.

"Look, Pat," she said somberly, "You need to come home now."

I thought about asking her why, but I instinctively knew better. I left the office to head home, stopping at the liquor store on my way to pick up a few beers. Back then, my favorite beer came in quart-sized bottles. I got back in the car and opened one of them, just for good measure. By the time I pulled into the driveway, both quarts were empty and I had a sufficient enough buzz to face whatever was coming, or so I thought.

As I walked in the front door, there stood Susan with a piece of paper in her hand and two black plastic trash bags at her feet. Inside those bags were all my worldly possessions.

"What's this?" I asked in an annoying tone.

"It's a court order—a restraining order."

"Wait? What?"

"You know *what*, Pat." I had seen her angry before, but never like this. She seemed less emotional and more resolved.

"But . . ."

Before I could offer my next objection, Susan interrupted, "You have thirty minutes to vacate this house. And if you refuse to go, the police will come and force you to leave."

There was nothing I could say. My drinking had been out of control for as long as I could remember—we both knew it, even though I was not yet ready to admit it. Those two garbage bags were appropriate representations of what I had done to my life and my marriage: I had trashed everything.

That was the beginning of the official end of my marriage.

TWO

How Many Times?

"How many times are you going to say you will stop, Pat?" This had become an all-too-familiar conversation between Susan and me. I loved her so much! I loved my children so much!

But I also *really* loved to drink.

I met Susan at a birthday party of a friend when we were both nineteen years old. We were having a good time at the party when I heard someone coming down the stairs to join us. Susan always disagrees with this part, but I contend that it is fully accurate. I raised my gaze to behold a beautiful girl descending the stairwell. She was wearing a tight sweater and had auburn hair that stretched almost past the length of her skirt (the short skirt is the part she disagrees with). That's how I remember it. I'm not a very dramatic person, but I kid you not when I say that before she had reached the bottom of those stairs, I knew that she was going to be my wife. Sometimes love at first sight really does happen.

We dated for a couple of years before getting married in 1976. Looking back, I can now see that I was an alcoholic long before we said I do. I thought that all my drinking was for fun—just to have a good time. But the truth is, I couldn't have a good time if we weren't drinking.

I can remember being at one of our family member's houses as a young married couple when I found out that there wasn't going to be any alcohol. I was furious. I made up my mind that I was going to be miserable because, after all, it wasn't a gathering worth attending if it was a gathering with no drinking.

This was my pattern everywhere we went. In fact, I would often slip outside and drink some beer while no one was looking. Up to the writing of this book, even Susan didn't know that I used to do that. Most of the time, however, sneaking outside wasn't necessary because most everyone we knew drank at every function we attended. When we met, we both drank as a social practice, but it meant much more to me than it did to Susan.

Rebecca was our first child, and I was working long hours to support the family. When Shawn came along two years later, I was working one full-time job, two part-time jobs, and was also taking twelve hours of college night classes at Saint Louis University. I was studying accounting and business management. Oddly enough, I almost flunked out of high school, but I became a mostly straight-A student in college.

Even so, with two young children at home, I just couldn't handle the workload, so I decided to take a semester off from school. Little did I know that I would never return to college. I began working in the accounting field, eventually finding my way into marketing and advertising. Things were changing all around us, as is common for that particular season of life. The only constant was my drinking.

I started hitting the bottle when I was twelve years old. I was staying at the house of a friend whose parents had a fully stocked bar. After we drank so much whiskey that they would certainly notice it was gone, we filled up the bottles with colored water so that no one would be the wiser. From there on out, alcohol was the staple in my life. I said it was all for fun, but I could have no fun without it.

ENOUGH

(A Glimpse from Susan's Perspective)

Dating Pat was so much fun—he was always the life of the party, and since we all drank, I guess I didn't realize that alcohol was never absent from anything we did. It just seemed like the thing to do when we were young and carefree. It seemed so harmless. And for many people, I suppose it is. I just didn't realize that Pat wasn't many people—he was an alcoholic.

Getting pregnant changed many of my youthful perspectives. I had a sense that as parents, it was time for us to grow up and put away some childish things. I decided that partying was no longer in the cards for me. I desired for Pat to feel the same, but that's not how it worked out.

In terms of working for our family, Pat was absolutely doing his best. He never missed a day of work, but he also never missed a day of drinking. He never let the alcohol ruin his job, but he was perfectly content to let it ruin his family. I was so grateful for his work ethic to support his family, but it was apparent that the drinking was no longer just for fun—it was now a full-fledged problem in our marriage.

While I stopped drinking regularly to try to be more present in our adult responsibilities, Pat began drinking even more, almost out of spite or some twisted principle to make up for both of us. He is a stubborn guy, which is one of his best attributes when it comes to so many important things. Back then, however, it was fast becoming a detriment to our relationship.

When I finally began speaking up and saying something about the drinking, he defied my wishes at every turn. In fact, the more I asked him to stop drinking so much, the more he drank to let me know that this was a nonnegotiable area for him. This stubborn defiance became a general attitude toward me. We were partners in so many things, but he let me know loud and clear that this particular part of his life was off limits to me. We were getting stuck. I could feel it happening, but there seemed to be nothing I could do about it.

Whether he realized it or not at the time, Pat's lifestyle of drinking was hurting everyone in our home. One night, his parents were coming over for dinner. I had worked hard all day to get the house ready and prepare the meal for *his* family, not to mention taking care of two little ones under the age of four. Later that evening, Pat's parents showed up, but Pat never did. He had gone out drinking again, skipping a meal with his own parents. He eventually arrived much later that night after they had left, drunk out of his mind. Our fights were becoming more predictably epic, but they weren't making a dent in the problem. He wasn't budging.

The final straw came when both the children got sick and developed pneumonia. I was running around in circles tending to two sick children and just hoping that my husband would walk through the door after work and help me with our family crisis. Five o'clock came and went. Then Six. Ten. Midnight. This time, he never came home.

At two o'clock in the morning, the phone rang. It was Pat calling from the police station. He had been pulled over for drunk driving and had been charged with a DWI (Driving While Intoxicated). He made a joke that he had been "driving with indigestion." I was not amused. It was a mess. It was an embarrassment. I was exhausted.

I was also his one phone call, but I was done. I hung up on him. Enough was enough. I had begged him long enough. It was time to stop talking about it and start moving towards making a change, even if it was a change that neither of us wanted in the big picture of the life we had planned together. I was heartbroken for our children and for myself, but I knew that this was never going to stop. Divorce had now become the only option, so after a long journey of pleading and trying, I gave up on our marriage and filed for divorce.

When things first became unbearable with his drinking, I set up a counseling appointment with our pastor. Pat reluctantly went along. The pastor was a licensed counselor for alcoholics, so I was hopeful that this would help. I was wrong. Pat recently shared with me that he remembers exactly what happened. He said that by the time we walked out of that counseling session, he had our pastor convinced that I was half-crazy and that there was nothing wrong with him. He was that persuasive—and at the time, he says that he considered it one of his crowning achievements.

I wasn't used to not knowing on any given night if my husband and the father of my children would actually come home or stay out drinking and driving and doing God knows what else. We lived in a state of constant fighting because I was always trying to get him to stop. Pat, on the other hand, seemed to use trouble as an opportunity to invite more trouble.

At one point, he tried to change and stopped drinking for about a month, but that month only revealed that drinking wasn't his only serious problem. Those thirty days were miserable, even with him sober. I literally couldn't live with or without his drinking . . . something had to change.

Our children were little, and I was carrying the load for the whole family. I didn't know what to do, so I began praying to God for help. I also went to see a divorce attorney, who gave me the advice of attending Al-Anon, a recovery group for families and friends of alcoholics. Oddly enough, it was this attorney's advice that began revealing God's answer to my simple prayer for help.

I gave my life to Christ when I was about eight years old, but I gradually grew away from the Lord, even though we were in church every Sunday. I was saved and God was up there somewhere, but it was never like He was doing anything in my life.

In Al-Anon, I met people who talked differently about God. It was the first time I had ever heard people speak about God truly working in their lives. I had no concept that a relationship with God could be accessible or personal. Because of their influence, I began seeking that kind of relationship with God for myself. I started reading things in the Bible like 1 Corinthians 13, the love chapter, and I knew in my heart that this was what I wanted for my life, my children, and my marriage. I knew that I was far away from that reality, so I just opened up my broken heart to God—to let His will be done in me because I knew that I could no longer live as I was.

Soon afterward, I filed for divorce.

After the divorce, I found a true community of friends at another church in town, a nondenominational church. They loved me and introduced me to even deeper aspects of a life with Jesus that I never knew could exist. I was a part of a singles small group with my new friends, and though everything in my life had been turned upside down, God was beginning to put me back together. The children also loved the church. We were a broken family, but we were beginning to experience healing in the middle of our brokenness.

The only thing missing from all this was my ex-husband, but I had given up on the idea of fixing him—that was beyond my ability or control.

Belonging

Even as Susan was kicking me (Pat) out of the house, I still thought that I could fix this. I'm very persuasive. I just knew that if I tried hard enough and invoked a little contrition or charm, I could change her mind. But I was wrong—she wasn't budging. This was happening whether I wanted it to or not.

I had passed the point of no return.

The night I left our house with my trash bags as suitcases, I went out and got absolutely sloppy, crawling drunk—

because, you know, after you just lost your family because of your drinking, getting drunk makes a ton of sense. I was addicted to all of it, both the drinking and to brashly tempting fate with its consequences. I woke up the next morning in my parents' basement, but I have no recollection of what happened that night or how I got there.

I was extremely hung over, but I tried to call Susan anyway. She wouldn't have anything to do with me. For the first time in my life, reality began to set in, and I began to accept the fact that I had a drinking problem. The realization came about six years too late. I had destroyed my marriage. I felt utterly hopeless, but little did I know that this experience of hopelessness was actually preparing me for a life I couldn't even dream of at this point in time—or at any point in time.

Feeling especially broken and desperate to win back my family, I went to my first meeting. Susan had suggested that I go to a treatment center for alcoholics, but there was no way that I could take thirty days off from work. Instead, I went to an AA meeting and learned that if you could go to ninety meetings in ninety days and not miss a day, it was the equivalent of completing a thirty-day treatment facility program. I thought this would help me to win her back.

I did it. I went to ninety meetings in ninety days. It began the process of me getting sober, but it also caused me to take an honest look at the rest of my life. I tried to tell Susan about my progress, but she still wouldn't back down on her decision.

Ninety days wasn't going to fix six years. It was a hard pill to swallow, but she followed through on her promise, and soon the divorce was finalized.

I was devastated on a personal front because I had lost my wife and only got to see my children for six hours every other weekend. I hated and resented Susan for what she was doing to me, not fully owning what I had done to her. Personally, things had completely fallen apart, but professionally, things were beginning to take off.

When we got married, we were dirt poor. We borrowed money from Susan's mom and dad every week to feed our family. But a few months after the divorce, I took a new job with a new startup marketing company. For whatever reason, I was very successful at this new company, and within six months, I was making more money than I had ever dreamed. I was able to pay child support to help my family, but I was still completely separated from them. The pain was so deep that I didn't know what to do with it, especially now that I couldn't just pour liquor into the void and hope it all washed away. I was now a sober mess of a person rather than the drunk mess I used to be. The crater that had always been inside of me was more evident than ever, but I still had no clue how to fill it or with what.

Since AA was a program that utilized spiritual principles, I began earnestly looking into spiritual things. I had gone to church the entire time I was married and drinking, but everything about it was a turnoff to me. I began exploring New Age philosophies—other ways to reach God outside of the stuffy, fake paradigms of religion that I had grown up with and had experienced in my marriage as an adult. I wanted nothing to do with church or church people.

I knew that Susan was going to a church, though. How could I not know? I would get the children every other weekend, and they would go on and on about this Tuesday night program at their church. I became convinced that Susan and the children had joined a cult, which made me resent her even more. Even so, I saw this as my chance to regain custody of my children. All I had to do was get more information on the cult and take it to a judge. I would be able to easily prove that Susan was endangering our children, and I would be awarded custody instead.

So one Sunday I told Susan that I was going to drop the children off at church and then come inside to attend with her. She had no idea that I planned to gather all the data I needed to convince a judge to take the children away from her.

I drove up to Grace Church in St. Louis only to find that there was a literal traffic jam to get into the parking lot. The line of cars seemed to stretch for a mile. It took forever to reach the drop-off location for the children. Then I had to drive way back out into the humongous parking lot to find a space. It was like going to a shopping mall—and it was the middle of July and extremely hot outside. I was sweating profusely by the time I walked back across the parking lot and reached the bottom of the steps leading up to the front door of the church. Susan was standing there with a very annoyed look on her face.

"You're late," she complained. I was so aggravated that I wanted to push her down those stairs, but I was on a mission, so cooler heads prevailed . . . for the moment.

When we walked into the sanctuary, I looked around to see several thousand people crammed in on all sides. TV cameras were stationed in various locations throughout the room. All of this just served to confirm my suspicions that this was a cult—more nails in the coffin of fake religion. The good news was that the weirder things became, the more evidence I would have to seek custody.

The only seats we could find together were in the middle of a long row, so we had to climb over a bunch of people to get to them. My frustration meter was reaching new levels. We finally found our seats and sat down, but only in time to be told that we had to stand up again for the singing. Meter rising.

But then something weird happened—just not in the way I had imagined. As everyone in that room began singing, raising their hands, and worshipping God, my perspective shifted. I began to really look at the people all around me. They were not who I had been expecting them to be. I saw young families and businessmen dressed in suits and ties—they didn't look like crazy people who would be at a cult. They seemed like people I would meet in the store or at the office. In fact, nobody in the church looked the way I had envisioned.

After worship ended, we all sat down, but then one guy stood up and began speaking out very loudly above the rest. It was weird to me, the kind of weirdness I was here to chronicle for my big plan. It's hard to describe, but as he began speaking, a hush fell across the room—and across me as well. Somewhere deep down inside, I knew that this was a message from God, even though I had never experienced anything like this before.

What felt like a thick mist suddenly came over me—like I was enveloped in a cloud. Then I heard someone speak in this cloud—he was speaking directly to me: "How many times do I have to call you?" He asked it three times. I later found out that these were the words the pastor was speaking from the stage, but from my perspective, I was hearing someone else—someone speaking specifically to me.

I had been searching for spiritual things, and at that point in my life, I considered myself a spiritual person. A good person. A happy person, minus the fact that I was missing my wife and children. But this was something so different—so much more all-consuming than any confidence I had in my own self or my spiritual pursuits. This experience completely wrecked all of that. It wrecked *me*.

When the cloud lifted, I discovered that I was sobbing uncontrollably. Here I was in the middle of a huge church that was pin-drop silent, and I couldn't stop crying to save my life.

I wasn't in a trance or anything like that. I was still completely aware of my own thoughts—in fact, my own brain was screaming at me, "You've lost your mind! What is wrong with you? Stop crying in front of these people right now!"

But I couldn't stop. Then the pastor said that he felt like he should invite anyone who wanted to answer Jesus' call to know Him as their personal Savior to come forward. I felt like a man in a desert who hadn't had a sip of water in a month and was offered a pitcher of ice water. I wanted it so badly!

But I still couldn't stop crying, and I was so embarrassed. I opted to stay put. Eventually, my emotions settled down and the church service continued. When it was over, Susan and I went our separate ways. We didn't discuss the fact that I had wept openly like a baby. I was too proud to acknowledge it. I had survived whatever *that* was and had made it out of that place with my dignity mostly intact.

I may not have been crying anymore, but something inside me wasn't right after that morning. From Sunday night all the way through Monday, I was miserable. Well, miserable isn't the most accurate description. I felt a deep and grave sense of loss—as if I had held a fortune in my hands, but then lost it. I sensed that I had forfeited something of great value. The opportunity had been mine to own it, but I had turned it down.

By Tuesday, the feeling still hadn't subsided. In fact, it was getting worse. I knew from my children that the church met on Tuesday nights, so that night, I went back. Susan always went on Tuesdays, so I let her know that I was coming. We sat together again.

To my relief, the pastor was once again wiling to offer the same invitation as Sunday. I was elated! It was as if I had squandered a huge pile of lottery winnings, but then, against all odds, I had won the lottery again two days later! This time, I didn't hesitate—what good are appearances when you are dying of thirst on the inside? I ran down front, fell on my knees, and gave my life to Christ.

THE HEAVY SENSE OF REGRET LIFTED, AND IT WAS REPLACED BY A SENSE OF FREEDOM, JOY, HAPPINESS, AND BELONGING.

As soon as I did, the heavy sense of regret lifted, and it was replaced by a sense of freedom, joy, happiness, and belonging. Truly, I had always struggled with that last one—to know where I belong in this world. But that night, I felt a sense of authentic belonging. I had come there planning to get my children back, but God had another plan in mind.

From Alone to Aware

At the moment Jesus came into my life, Susan and I had been divorced for over a year and a half. I thought *that* was my biggest problem, but it wasn't really the root issue. I had tried to stubbornly make my own way in life, and it had led me to financial success but personal failure. Alcohol was just one component of my real problem—trying to control my own life all by myself.

I didn't want to go it alone anymore.

Susan had been part of a singles' Bible study at church. We had no idea that earlier that week, seven or eight of them had decided to go to the same service at church that Sunday so they could sit together. The group rarely sat together in the same service because they each came at the times convenient for their schedules. But for some reason, they really wanted to sit together that particular Sunday.

When we walked in, they were already sitting in their seats—again, we were late because of my sweaty trek through sector seven-niner of the church parking lot. We sat down about four rows in front of them. Later on, every one of them told us that the minute they saw us, they each had the strongest impression to pray for us. They didn't discuss this among themselves at the time, but they each began praying for us on their own. They obviously knew Susan, but they had never seen me, though they knew I was her ex-husband.

That was 1984. We remarried in 1985. That makes Susan both my first wife and my second wife. This time, the groom that walked down the aisle to meet his bride was a different person—not perfect, but not stubbornly trying to be in charge of his own story. I had given up being in control, though I still sometimes want to wrestle it back. Jesus had my full heart—and Susan and our children had my full devotion as a husband and father.

A final significant thing occurred that Tuesday night in 1984. On my way out of the church, I noticed a bookstore, so I stopped in to see what was there. I didn't own a Bible yet, but my eyes were drawn elsewhere—to an endcap display for a book entitled *God's Smuggler*. The title intrigued me, even though the author's name seemed a bit foreign to me: Brother Andrew. Regardless, the term "smuggler" piqued my curiosity not just in an intellectual way, but somewhere deeper in a place I couldn't yet identify.

I bought a copy and took it home to my condo. I lived there alone, but that night, I didn't feel alone. I couldn't put the book down. I read until three o'clock in the morning before grabbing a few hours of sleep and heading to the office. The next night, I did the same thing and finished the book.

When I got done, I prayed a very simple prayer—the only kind of prayer I knew how to pray. I now see that it is the best kind of prayer. "God, if You ever want to use me to help like this guy does, I am making myself available to You." And that was that. From that moment forward, I had a hunger to learn about Christian persecution. I began devouring every book I could find on the subject.

Four years later, I would find myself standing at the Russian border holding two suitcases filled with Bibles and worship tapes. It was contraband—and I was ready to smuggle it across the border for the sake of the One who had literally saved my life and my marriage. How many times had I come home drunk, or not come home until the next day? How many times had I committed to change? How many times had I failed? The answers to each of these would be hard to measure. They are too many to count.

But how many times did God have to call me to a place of belonging so I could discover who I really was and what He actually wanted to do with my life? I don't know how many times He called, but I know that answering Him once was enough—enough for grace to change everything.

THREE

What Would You Dare to Do?

South Sudan

From that moment in the middle of nowhere when I looked back over my shoulder at those devastated Sudanese people still on the run from an ever-approaching enemy, things were never the same for me. We had no idea where the money was going to come from, but we began telling people back home about what we were seeing—and that we were refusing to sit and do nothing about it.

Sure enough, people responded with generosity, a little bit at a time. It was enough to take another trip back to South Sudan to keep trying to figure out ways to bring food and relief to people being devastated by the civil war around them. I met a couple guys there who were interested in working in South Sudan, one of whom was already engaged there in relief efforts. We began planning ways to work as a team.

We picked a date in September and met in Nairobi, Kenya. We pooled our resources and came up with enough money to provide four thousand people with a two-pound bag of rice. Since others had given us money to accomplish this mission, I wanted to be able to come home and tell them all about how we delivered on our promise. However, the trip didn't work out according to my best-laid plans.

It was the rainy season, and three times, we prepared to take off in the airplane full of supplies, but the weather made it impossible. I was so frustrated! We couldn't reach the people we had come to help. On the last day, we were able to take off, but the pilot received a radio message in the air that it was too muddy to land. We had to turn back.

I returned home having never delivered the food. I didn't have any grand stories to tell. I felt like a failure because I had not been accountable to those who had sent us. The next week, someone else was finally able to deliver the food, but that first trip began to teach me that things wouldn't always work out according to my plans. I had to trust a plan higher than my own.

Over the next year, we did another two or three trips to South Sudan and our work continued to expand so much that we were growing beyond the scope of ICC (International Christian Concern), the organization we were working under at the time. They really weren't outfitted to be heavily involved in humanitarian aid on this level. They were doing incredible work, but this was not their specific targeted mission.

As you know, a year later found me in an undisclosed border town between Afghanistan and Pakistan preparing to do some of our first relief work with refugees there. We were outside our hotel around midnight when I heard God speak to my heart, "I want you to start another organization." Now, God had already done so much in my life, and everything He had said up to this point had been nothing less than transformational, but as you know, I'm stubborn. Heading into a war zone was one thing, but starting my own nonprofit felt much, much more difficult. I did not believe that the world needed another nonprofit organization.

I told God no. I kid you not, that's what I did. I began mansplaining to the Divine about how busy I was and how I had no interest in all the administration and the other less desirable parts of leading an actual nonprofit. I just wanted to help people, not become a paper pusher or a money counter. After all, I reasoned within myself, the *last* thing the world needed was another organization.

God ignored my protests. He continued speaking as if I had said nothing, and as if He wasn't at all offended by my resistance. He said that He wanted me to start an organization, but that He didn't want me to model it after others. "I'm going to do a new work through you." I had no idea what He was talking about. What part of "I will do anything for love, but I won't do *that*" did He not understand? I kept making excuses. He kept giving directions. This went on for a while.

Ultimately, I learned that if you have an argument with God, you're probably going to lose. I did, anyway. After I made it home from that trip, I began reaching out to some friends and we formed a makeshift exploratory board. They were kind enough to do a lot of the footwork regarding what it would take to incorporate and organize appropriately. On February 13, 2002, International Crisis Aid (ICA) was officially incorporated and soon thereafter received tax-exempt status from the IRS.

God had spoken, regardless of my protests, and Crisis Aid was born.

Trading Lives for Oil

The bonfire of violence, poverty, and death that was raging in Sudan seemed so vast and out of control that anything we tried to do felt overwhelmingly insufficient. If you've ever seen an aerial view of one of the devastating wildfires in the Pacific Northwest that stretches for literally thousands upon thousands of acres, then you've probably seen what it looks like when an airplane drops a load of water into the blazing abyss. It seems like it does nothing, and it would be easy to think, "What's the point? These problems are so huge that whatever I do won't make a difference!"

Those aerial views can't adequately capture the physical and emotional loss that individuals and communities are experiencing on the ground. When a person loses their house or a neighborhood loses an entire street of houses, and when once-secure people are now sleeping in homeless shelters in high school gymnasiums or community centers, the view from below is quite different.

Now imagine what it's like to zero in on a single person or family who just lost everything. They are hungry or hurt or panicked because they can't reach another friend or family member who was near the fire. They have soot all over their clothes, bodies, and faces. They reek of smoke. They don't just need another metaphorical bucket of water dumped on their fire to try to fix the bigger problem; they also need words of compassion, a place to sleep safely, a meal to eat, and partners to help them rebuild their lives. It can be overwhelming to engage individuals—real people—and not just the bigger problems of a surrounding society at large. It's hard to not just dump more water, but to also walk with the people who have lost everything through their first or next steps of survival.

I knew the situation in Sudan was a fire that we couldn't put out, but that did not mean that we shouldn't rush to the aid of those who had lost everything, including hope. I don't mean "hope" as some cliché. Losing hope is something that people and communities sometimes never recover from. As our stories will reveal, it can begin a vicious cycle of living that is devoid of any real life. Eventually people stop reaching for that which might help them. They often stop reaching altogether.

Just ask someone in the United States who once worked a lucrative job, but now lives on the street, and they will probably tell you that they suffered the loss of more than just a good job or income. Somewhere along the way, enough fires burned up enough parts of their personal and professional lives that they lost the ability to keep reaching for the next rung of survival.

There are definitely vast differences affecting poverty in America and overseas, but loss, pain, and hopelessness are universal. More importantly, the response to hopelessness from a gospel perspective is universally clear: be like Jesus, who not only saw the problem, but humbled Himself and intentionally inserted Himself into the problem with those who were suffering from it. Put on their shoes like He did. Don't just watch them in the fire, but rather walk in the fire with them, as God did with three Hebrew slaves who refused to bow their lives to their emperor's false god (Daniel 3).

Paul writes about Christ's willingness to feel the heat of humanity's tragedy and shows us the way to do likewise: "Don't look out only for your own interests, but take an interest in others, too. You must have the same attitude that Christ Jesus had. Though he was God, he did not think of equality with God as something to cling to. Instead, he gave up his divine privileges; he took the humble position of a slave and was born as a human being. When he appeared in human form, he humbled himself in obedience to God and died a criminal's death on a cross" (Philippians 2:4-8).

His mission was clear: join the ones He cared for in whatever state they were in.

Of course, I'm not Jesus. When I really began trying to figure out how to join and help those who were suffering in Sudan, it felt completely undoable. I doubted not only myself, but also whether or not I had actually heard from God. Yes, He had already proven that He was with me multiple times, but I bet I'm not the only person who still doubts Him when the next impossibility emerges.

The situation in Sudan was unworkable. The civil war between the government of the north and the resistance forces in the south had started off as a religious war. Northern Sudan was predominately Muslim, while the south was filled with people who were more likely to be either Christian or to hold an animist religious viewpoint. *Animism* is the belief that objects, places, and creatures all possess a distinct spiritual essence. Animists perceive that all things—animals, plants, rocks, rivers, weather systems, human handiwork, and perhaps even words—are somehow actually animated and alive.

The war started for religious reasons, but once oil was discovered in South Sudan, the conflict became more a matter of clearing and seizing valuable oil fields than anything else.

> HIS MISSION WAS CLEAR: JOIN THE ONES HE CARED FOR IN WHATEVER STATE THEY WERE IN.

Religion became a convenient excuse for nationalistic greed, and thus unspeakable violence became not only acceptable, but also government mandated. Ethnic cleansing and all its accompanying atrocities were the quickest path to clear oil fields of the pesky humans who occupied these profit-rich properties. Even in the West, this is often a strategy used by politicians or ideological tribal leaders: dehumanize one's opponent so you can treat them in any manner you choose without a second thought or any hesitation. It doesn't always end in ethnic cleansing, but it does always make doing the wrong thing appear seemingly right to those doing it.

When we were in Sudan, we would generally walk ten or fifteen miles every week to find those in need or to assess the ongoing damage for future relief efforts. We came across more destroyed villages than I can recount—whole communities completely burned to the ground. Often, all around the charred rubble were little flags positioned in perfectly surveyed squares. They were already staking out their oil fields, trading human life for profit.

Imagine this was happening in your town or city. Put yourself into the shoes of someone foreign to your context. Imagine with me that St. Louis is under attack by the government. Imagine that all of the major buildings have been bombed out and whole neighborhoods have been leveled and burned, many men killed and many wives and daughters raped and left for dead. Imagine that you have only seconds to attempt to muster up your family in the middle of the night in your underwear so that you can run for your life on foot into the surrounding woods around your house. You hear screams, gunshots, and explosions in the distance. You are barefoot, as is your twelve-year-old daughter whom you are desperately trying to keep from screaming in terror, thus giving away your position.

These are almost unimaginable scenarios for many of us, but this exact situation was reality for millions of Sudanese families in the south. They would flee and run as far as they could, but there was no place that was completely safe for them—all the adjacent villages were either destroyed or facing imminent attack. Besides all this, the surrounding villages were already short on food and resources.

I remember coming upon a group of people we found after about six or seven hours of walking from where their village had once stood. It was blisteringly hot, and we had walked through thick African bush—a jungle with a very narrow path snaking through it. The trees in this particular area were covered in huge, sharp thorns. Walking among these trees took time because if we were to just haphazardly walk or run, they would rip us up to bloody shreds.

We found several hundred people living beneath these trees, hoping that their distance into this seemingly God-forsaken place would deter the pursuit of their brutal attackers. What kind of terror and desperation would cause people to hide under thorn trees? They were cut and bleeding from their own hasty journey into the bush, but all this was better than the alternative. They were being hunted by the Sudanese government.

What would you do in this situation? What kind of dent could you make in the madness? All we could do was spend time with them in their pain, give them what little food we had, and tell them that God saw their pain and had sent us there to help. Then we had to leave, hoping to return soon with more supplies—if, that is, they could survive long enough to receive them.

A Nun's Underwear Drawer and a Billboard

Going back and forth between Sudan and the United States often left my mind tired and reeling from all that I was witnessing. I wasn't lacking hope, and I felt confident that helping one person or one village at a time was worth the effort. But I felt a sense of insecurity—that I had no business doing any of this in the first place. Surely someone else could do it better than a formerly divorced recovering alcoholic in advertising. I knew I had heard from God, but I still questioned Him every day—well, mainly I questioned myself before Him.

I asked myself so many times what I was doing there. I was neither qualified, nor did I deserve the incredible privilege of being in these places to help people—especially during those early years.

Maybe you can relate.

After one of our initial research trips to Sudan, I came home and learned of a conference on Sudan being held at a convent in Indiana. There were going to be experts on Sudan telling us what was going on and what we could do about it. I was already busy trying to raise awareness and funds, so this seemed liked a great opportunity to learn and to network for future endeavors.

When I arrived at the convent, we were assigned rooms— nuns' bedrooms, to be exact. I have been a lot of strange places and experienced many strange things, but this was one of the most uncomfortable and weirdest of all my experiences. As I was unpacking my bag to put my things into the little chest of drawers, I remember wondering if I would open it to find a nun's underwear. Thankfully, the drawer was empty.

Unfortunately, so was the content of the conference.

The experts on the panel were supposed to know everything about what was going on in Sudan, but after a while, it became apparent that not one of them had ever actually been there. Not one. It was also evident to me that most of what they were saying was inaccurate. Between sessions, I tried to pull them aside and talk to them about what I had seen and experienced from meeting people and working on the ground in Sudan, but they were not interested in hearing anything I had to say. This just reinforced the feelings I have always fought—that since I'm not a pastor or a missionary, I don't belong in their group. I'm too rough around the edges.

I was severely discouraged. If you can't even get "experts" in ministry to listen or help, what's the point of trying?

I found myself back in my nun's room, sitting in a funk. After sulking for a while, I guiltily opened my Bible, figuring that I should probably do something spiritual. I randomly opened my Bible to Isaiah 58. (Random reading is not something I advocate for as a regular Bible study method—it was just what happened to me that day.)

YOU CAN SHARE A HOPE HIGHER THAN ANY OF OUR SITUATIONS.

As I read, something strange happened. It seemed as if verses six through twelve somehow lifted off the page. According to my visual perception, it was like I saw those verses up in the air and the rest of the Bible beneath them. Some might call it a vision, but I'm not sure. What was clear was that God was trying to get my attention. He was saying to me the same thing I want to pass along to you as you hear the stories of people who may not share your geography or your life situation, but with whom you can share a hope higher than any of our situations.

"Is not this the kind of fasting I have chosen:
to loose the chains of injustice
    and untie the cords of the yoke,
to set the oppressed free
    and break every yoke?
Is it not to share your food with the hungry
    and to provide the poor wanderer with shelter—
when you see the naked, to clothe them,
    and not to turn away from your own flesh and blood?
Then your light will break forth like the dawn,
    and your healing will quickly appear;
then your righteousness will go before you,
    and the glory of the Lord will be your rear guard.
Then you will call, and the Lord will answer;
    you will cry for help, and he will say: Here am I.
If you do away with the yoke of oppression,
    with the pointing finger and malicious talk,
and if you spend yourselves in behalf of the hungry
    and satisfy the needs of the oppressed,
then your light will rise in the darkness,
    and your night will become like the noonday.
The Lord will guide you always;
    he will satisfy your needs in a sun-scorched land
    and will strengthen your frame.
You will be like a well-watered garden,
    like a spring whose waters never fail.

Your people will rebuild the ancient ruins
    and will raise up the age-old foundations;
you will be called Repairer of Broken Walls,
    Restorer of Streets with Dwellings."
(Isaiah 58:6-12, NIV)

I knew that these words were confirmation that I was going in the right direction, regardless of what anyone else was doing or thought about what I was doing. A few weeks later, a lady walked up to me at a church and told me that she felt God directing her to give me a verse. It was from Isaiah 58.

Just as it says in Isaiah, when you're doing God's work and you lose heart, you will be able to "call, and the LORD will answer." To "cry for help, and he will say: Here am I." Another time early on, I was back in that same old place of doubting. I know what you're thinking: *Geeze, Pat, how much does God have to do before you'll trust Him?* In my experience, most people who are pursuing heroic endeavors to put out endless fires of poverty or violence need to be constantly encouraged by God because the flames are so hot and encroaching—and they know they are powerless on their own to do anything about it that can succeed or last.

It was during the first year of my trips to Sudan. I was back home and on my way to the Lake of the Ozarks to meet Susan and the children for a little getaway. My heart was deeply wrestling with everything going on when I passed a billboard that caught my eye. It was green with white letters, and it read, "What would you dare to do for me if you knew you could not fail?" Below, it was signed "Jesus Christ."

I'd seen religious billboards before, and some that even quoted God in such a manner, but this particular message hit home for me—so much so that I pulled off the next exit of the highway and circled back the other direction to a previous exit so I could get back on the highway and see it again. But I couldn't find it. I figured that I must not have gone far enough back, so I circled back again, going several more exits this time just to make sure. I repeated this same sequence two or three times, but to this day, I have never again seen that billboard. I honestly believe that it was God answering my inward cries, just as He said He would in Isaiah 58, with both comfort and a challenging reminder to trust Him for what was ahead rather than worrying about my own inabilities.

As always, He gave me just what I needed to not only keep going, but to push the boundaries of what we were doing. This time, it was a reminder that this wasn't about *me* or even my confidence or perception of who I was in ministry. This was about *them*—the oppressed, naked, homeless, hungry, and afflicted. They were where God's heart lay, so that's where I needed to continue to go.

Flying Closer to the Fire

As our trips to Sudan grew in number, so did our knowledge of where the most desperate people were. As I said before, we often enter situations not knowing where we will end up. The way we figure it out is to find out where the UN or other relief agencies are not willing or able to go—that's where we try to set up our operations. We figure these kinds of places will always be near the epicenter of the greatest needs.

As things escalated in Sudan, the government set up no-fly zones, forbidding unauthorized travelers from entering certain parts of the country. These were areas where government forces were attacking civilians and destroying villages. With the government trying to stop anyone from getting into these areas, we had to get creative. We began acting as if it was impossible for us to fail. After all, that was what God had said was the case.

We chartered some old Antonov An-12 Russian bombers to fly us where we needed to go. We had to fly below radar and land in fields so narrow that, quite honestly, it seemed that it would be difficult to land a bicycle. These locations were usually three or hours from where we needed to be. We would be dropped off with our food and had to reach out to our contacts from there, sometimes walking for hours to get to them. Just transporting the food to the right locations took several hours. Those were crazy days with huge logistical challenges on all sides.

But it was always about the people—and some needed us more than others.

Once, we found ourselves at a Doctors Without Borders (MSF) camp in South Sudan. I noticed a woman sitting in one of the makeshift clinic rooms with a baby lying beside her. The poor baby's stomach was so large that it looked like he had swallowed a basketball. When I asked the doctors about it, they said that the baby had some kind of cancer and was going to die. There was nothing they could do.

This camp was hundreds of miles from the woman's home, so she was far from any kind of support system. The doctors told me that she was just sitting there waiting for her child to die so she could walk back home. The journey was too long to carry a child who was that sick.

"How long has she been here?" I asked.

"About a week now," replied the doctor.

"When do you expect the baby to die?"

He looked off into the distance. "Well, it could be any day, or it could be another two weeks. There's really no way to tell."

I put myself into her shoes. My God! Can you even imagine being all alone, hundreds of miles from home, with no transportation, just watching and waiting for your precious child to die from cancer so you can walk alone across a dangerous war zone to rejoin your family and begin to mourn your incalculable loss? I thought of my own children. Once again, doing nothing was not an option.

This woman needed to be back with her family so she could have some semblance of dignity and support. We began asking around and found out how to get to her village. When our charter plane arrived the next day, we asked the pilot to take us there so we could take some food and supplies, but more importantly, so we could deliver the mother and her dying child back to her community. The pilot agreed and we took off—I will never forget one of the doctors telling us that they hoped the child didn't die before we got there. The situation was beyond heartbreaking.

Forces supported by the GOS (Government of Sudan) had recently attacked this mother's village, and it was believed they had left the area. We were going there to spend the night and distribute the remaining aid, having the plane return the following afternoon with another full load of food and aid to pick us up.

While en route, the pilot received a message via radio that the village was most likely going to be attacked again within the next twenty-four hours. We had no idea how he came across this information, but apparently there was still a large contingent of GOS soldiers on the outskirts of this village. We were strongly advised not to land and to definitely not spend the night there.

The pilot wanted to turn around, but we kept pushing him until he reluctantly agreed to continue on. We discussed the options, but we decided that we could not take the mother and child to another area where they would be with strangers. Delivering them to their family was still the right thing to do. Yes, we knew that we were delivering this woman into possible danger, but she was begging us to take her home—danger was not something she could escape in any place we could take her. She would rather be with family when the baby died than be all alone.

I held the baby on the plane ride. His stomach was hard as a rock. I was devastated for his family. We had radioed ahead to let the village elders know that we were coming and that we were bringing the mother and her child. When we landed, they were waiting for us. The pilot said that it had to be a true drop and go—we were not staying on the ground very long, not even long enough to turn off the propellers.

Upon landing, things went into high gear. It was the quickest I have ever seen a plane unloaded and aid carried off by the people. As I helped the mother and her child out of the plane, loud gusts of air blew all around us from the propellers. The family of the dying baby rushed to her and began weeping. The father gently took the little boy into his arms and raised him to his shoulders as they quickly retreated to a safer spot. The mother looked back at us without saying anything. We couldn't speak each other's language, but as our eyes met, I could see the immense gratitude in her heart.

The desperation was palpable. Knowing that the government forces could attack that night was heartbreaking. It was another one of those times when I just said in my heart, *God, what am I even doing here? I'm just an advertising executive— and now I'm taking a strange woman to this strange place, with government forces closing in on us.* But I also had the opposing thought: someone had to get this mother and her child back to her family. I wish I could have fixed their whole situation—the poverty, the cancer, and the violence. I couldn't. On that day, God's work for us was to show His love, the best we could, to one person in one village in extreme need.

Per our agreement with the pilot, we soon took off and flew away from what seemed like a foreign world, even for the people of South Sudan. The geography was vast, as were the unique situations and needs. Who knows how many other similar situations of desperation and need were happening all over the country—and for that matter, all over the world?

I was never able to follow up with that mother and her family. War doesn't always allow such things. But on that one day, in that one crisis among billions in a dark and fallen world where violence and abuse abounds, I was able to tell one woman that God cared about what was happening to her. He truly did—so much that He sent His only Son to pay the price to someday fully redeem what was causing all the suffering she was experiencing. He also loved her enough to send a complete stranger like me to help—someone to whom others had given money and supplies so I could be there for her in her despair. God knew her name. He knew her baby's name. No matter what happened, He wanted her to know that there was hope.

That day, one person heard about hope—and for that one day, though nothing we could do was enough to stop the blazing fire, one person knowing that she had been seen and loved by God was our mission on this earth. We are merely one glass of water, but we are not just poured out on an endless fire. Rather, God shows us one thirsty person at a time and invites us to offer them living water. God is making all things right. He will make sure that nothing is wasted in the end. Through shouts and bombs and sickness and death, He is still whispering and working, and He won't stop until He has completed His good work.

FOUR

Giving Up
Is Not an Option

South Sudan

"The orphans from the village were stolen—they're slaves now."

It was a phone call I will never forget, and one that would change the course of multiple lives, including my own. This is a story that, at one point in my life, I vowed to never tell publicly. But I think it will soon become clear why I changed my mind. This is also the story of how I met two men who have become lifelong friends—Dane Welch and Dave Bennett. Without their help, this story would most likely not have turned out like it did.

Our relief work in South Sudan was ongoing, as were the civil war and the atrocities that came along with it. One day, ICC received a phone call about a guy in Texas who had somehow come across critical news: There was a group of twenty-one orphans who had been captured by GOS forces after a raid left their village destroyed and all of their parents murdered. The government soldiers had brought them up north, where they lived as slaves. This was actually a fairly common occurrence during the war; the government would capture people and sell them into slave markets.

One of the underground churches, a Dinka church, had raised money and had bought back all twenty-one of them from their owners. This community was raising these children under the radar, but the GOS somehow found out that the oldest child had turned seventeen, the age at which children were conscripted into the army. With this change, the GOS began looking for all the children so they could take them back into their custody. They were in danger and needed to get out of Sudan before they were captured again.

This information had found its way to me through a winding back channel of underground churches meeting in Sudan's capital city of Khartoum. One of the pastors in this secret network had somehow met the orphans, and their story had made it all the way to Texas and back to us. The contact in Texas told me the horrendous story and then asked a heroic question: "We are trying to get them out—do you think you could help?"

Once again, this was something we had no business engaging with, but for this moment, what greater epicenter of destruction existed than twenty-one children being sold into slavery after the death of their parents? I knew in my heart that we needed to make our way to the worst and see what God would do when we got there.

"Let's do it."

Using his resources and back channels, this guy was making arrangements to have them transported from Khartoum to the Egyptian border and into Cairo. If we could get them to Cairo, they would be rescued and we could work to help them begin finding new lives outside of the atrocities of the Sudanese war. He was paying for everything, and the dates were set for the exchange. My role was to meet them at the Egyptian border and bring them into Cairo. Everything was set.

The day of our operation arrived, and I was about to leave for Egypt when the phone in my office rang. This part is sensitive, so I can't really tell you who it was, except that it was an organization with ties to diplomacy and intelligence. He told me that they knew all about my upcoming trip to Cairo. They knew about the orphans. They knew everything.

"You need to understand something," the man on the phone stated grimly. "There is a big problem with all of this. The government of Sudan has somehow found out about your plans, and they have contacted us. They are threatening to make this an international incident."

I was stunned and didn't know what to say.

"Should you go forward with trying to rescue these children, it would provide proof to the world that slavery is really going on in Sudan. Furthermore, we fear for your life because there have been veiled threats by the GOS to come after you to stop this. The government of Sudan does not want this to happen."

He said that some of their people wanted to meet with me in person to discuss the matter in greater detail. I agreed. He then concluded our conversation, but offered one more thought. "Off the record, we are a hundred percent behind you and applaud you for what you're doing." I told him that I appreciated the call.

He already knew that I was going to be staying at the Marriott in Cairo, something I had not told him. He told me to meet his people at the front desk at a certain time. I landed in Cairo later that night and proceeded to the hotel lobby the next morning as planned. A woman walked up to me.

"Mr. Bradley?"

"Yeah?"

"Come with me." She then explained who she was, and we walked rather quickly out of the hotel and got into a van that was waiting for us. For a few minutes she made small talk, asking me about my flight and my room.

Then she asked, "Do you notice anything peculiar about this van?"

"As a matter of fact, I do." I replied. "It's pretty bulky and there are no windows."

"Well," she said, "that's because this van is bomb proof." She wanted to make her next sentence hit home for me. "Mr.

Bradley, there are very credible threats against your life right here in Cairo—the government of Sudan has agents here as well. We're taking all possible precautions to protect you."

"Okay," I stammered. "Thank you, but where are we going?"

"We're taking you to the UN—well, the UNHCR." The UNHCR is the UN arm mandated to aid and protect refugees, forcibly displaced communities, and stateless people. They assist in their voluntary repatriation, local integration, or resettlement to a third country. She told me that they were taking me to meet the person in charge of these matters for Northern Africa.

"We'll be walking you directly into the office to keep you safe, but you need to understand something before you talk to them."

"What's that?"

"They think that you're trying to smuggle children. They don't understand the reason behind what you're trying to do. All they know is that you're trying to sneak some children out of South Sudan." She paused. "You see, we can't tell them what's going on because we're not supposed to be involved in this at all."

I told her that I understood, and soon we arrived at the UNHCR headquarters. The agent was right: they obviously thought the worst of me, because the reception I received was very cold and dismissive. They looked at me like I was scum—a child enslaver.

I was taken to the head official's office, and she treated me much the same. Finally I was able to tell them what was actually going on. I told them all about the work of Crisis Aid in Sudan and what we were trying to accomplish in rescuing the orphans. God gave us favor with her—her whole countenance changed, and it suddenly felt like I was in a different office in a completely different building.

"You know what, Mr. Bradley," she said, "I'm going to take this case on personally myself. Let's see if we can help get this thing resolved."

"Thank you so much," I replied.

"Your job is to get those children to me. I cannot get involved until you bring them here and turn them over to the UNHCR." I agreed, and we made arrangements for all of this to happen a few days later, which was when the children were slated to arrive at the border.

I had come alone to Cairo. My plan was to drive three or four hours to the border to meet the guy who was smuggling the children out. I had been told that the border guards had been paid off and would let the children through. The plan seemed set, but on the morning it was all supposed to go down, I received another phone call. The children had been discovered while the underground church contact was transporting them across country. The driver had been horribly tortured and was near death. And the government had taken the twenty-one orphaned slaves and put them in prison.

Smuggling Humans and Hope

His words were a gut punch, but in some ways I wasn't surprised. After all, I knew that someone in government knew what we were trying to do. Even so, the way things work is usually so chaotic and crooked that as long as you can get the right money to the right people at the right time, anything can get "lost in the mix" and turn out in your favor.

Unless you get killed, that is.

The situation had gone from bad to worse for these poor orphaned slaves, but we couldn't give up on them now, even if all hope seemed lost. The heroes in the Sudanese underground church were not yet done believing that God was going to fight for them and help them free these children. They were undeterred by the torture of one of their own for the cause of Christ. Soon, they made more contacts in the prison and once again formulated a price and a plan to sneak the children out and get them to the border.

For about three days, we were in the middle of planning and negotiating to make all this happen. One night at about 5:00 p.m., I received a phone call a pastor I had never met from the underground church network. He said enough about our plans that I believed he was who he said he was. He was calling to tell me that my life was in great danger that very night. He told me that I needed to get to the airport immediately and take the 8:00 p.m. flight back to the United States. He begged me to leave for the sake of my life. Then he hung up.

It's hard to describe what you feel after a call like this, but it all seemed so surreal. I walked out onto the balcony of my hotel room and sat down to think things through. Besides a few agencies, no one really knew exactly where I was or what I was doing. My wife knew that I was in Cairo and that it had something to do with orphans. That was it.

Then I realized that I was sitting on a balcony out in the open in a city where people were intent on killing me. That wasn't a smart move, so I went back inside the room. I contemplated what the man had told me and thought about leaving—no one would fault me for doing so. But then suddenly a light bulb went off in my head, granting instant clarity. I had come here for a reason—God had sent me to get something done. I knew that I couldn't leave until it was done.

Who else could meet those children? I was the one with the contacts at the UN, and I was the one they were expecting to bring them to safety. All around us were people we couldn't trust, and it was very possible that if I didn't get the children to the UN, they would be taken right back into Sudan. I wouldn't call my time in that hotel room a prayer time—it was more like I just got back on the same page with God, which I suppose is the best kind of prayer.

It was a long night because I was genuinely afraid for my life. But honestly, I was more scared of what might happen to those children if I left. My enemies knew where I was staying, though the Marriott was considered a secure hotel location for

Westerners. With all the strange phone calls and windowless vans, it felt like a story that no one would ever believe.

But it was happening.

No one busted through my door that night to kill me, and eventually the sun made its especially welcome return. I had survived the darkness, though I wasn't out of danger—it just felt better in the light. It was a reminder that just because everything seems hopeless, you don't have to give up. If you really believe God has put you somewhere for a reason, then it's on Him to take care of you. Sometimes you've got to stay in the place where if He doesn't show up, all will be lost.

IF YOU REALLY BELIEVE GOD HAS PUT YOU SOMEWHERE FOR A REASON, THEN IT'S ON HIM TO TAKE CARE OF YOU.

One of our common sayings among the team at Crisis Aid is *giving up is not an option*. We kept working over the next several days until one afternoon, I received word that the orphans had been removed from the jail and were on their way to the border. I was also told that I should not meet them at the border because of the ongoing intelligence chatter about threats to my life. The word out of South Sudan was that they had officially put a hit on me—a contract on my life. The truth of this was anyone's guess.

I don't know if the Sudanese agents knew what was happening with the orphans, but they were most definitely keeping an eye on me. This meant that if I showed up at the border, I might tip off the GOS agents that the orphans were there. They had suffered enough—I would not let them be collateral damage in this mess. I needed to deliver them to the UN, but I would have to meet them after they had crossed the border. That was the best way to keep them safe.

A friend who worked with us in the area—one of the pastors living in Cairo along with roughly two million other Sudanese refugees—courageously agreed to pick them up at the border and bring them to me so that I could bring them to the UN.

Then another call came—the children had arrived at the border, and if someone didn't show up soon to retrieve them, they would be forced to go back into Sudan. We knew that this was our last chance. My friend raced to meet them, and in a few hours, I saw the van pull up and I was finally able to see the children in person.

It was quite the sight—all twenty-one kids crammed into one van. When they emerged, they looked absolutely horrible, as you can imagine. There were expressions of despair and hopelessness on their faces, etched there by the horrors they had seen and experienced. I know it sounds strange to say, but when they saw me, a Westerner, a look of relief began to cascade across their faces because they knew that this was for real—they had made it out alive. Someone who looked like me would have never been allowed anywhere near where they were being enslaved and imprisoned.

It felt like we somehow already knew each other. I believe it was the Spirit of God bringing comfort—letting them know that they were going to be cared for and safe. By not giving up, we had the privilege of seeing those children come out of that van alive. It would take the UN some time to process them, which meant that they would be staying with the other Sudanese refugees in the ghettos. But to these orphans who had been in slavery and then prison, the ghettos of Cairo were like Beverly Hills.

After I connected the orphans with the UN, I was able to spend several days with them, learning about their lives and hearing their stories. I will never forget the story of a seven-year-old boy whose village was made up of families living in mud and grass huts. When the soldiers attacked, his father and mother ran out of the hut to see what was happening. They were met by a soldier with a sword—and he decapitated them both right there in front of this child. Then they grabbed him and took him into brutal slavery.

How would he ever get over this? I didn't know, but I knew that putting my hope in only what we could do was not enough. He would need something higher—and that higher Source of hope was the reason we were all together in the first place.

The UN had promised something unheard of: They would fast track these children into the adoption process, helping them get adopted in the US within six months. They meant well, but it didn't work out that way. All told, we began a two-year odyssey of trying to get them out of Cairo. Eventually, all but one of the orphans left Cairo and came to the United States as unaccompanied minor refugees, where they were resettled by a faith-based agency. The one who stayed in Cairo had met and married a guy in the Sudanese refugee camp, so she obviously wanted to stay there as she built a new family.

The reason I swore that I would never tell this story publicly was that I didn't want to mess with the new lives these children were building in America. I didn't want reporters and journalists trying to track them down or badgering them for details about this incredible story. There have been people over the years who have heard it off the record and expressed interest in writing articles or making movies about it, but I've always said no.

Now I'm willing to share it because all of the children are grown. I want their stories to be heard, their lives to be honored, and God to be glorified for what He has done. I don't know all of the details of everything that happened to them since they made it out of Cairo, but for all of my doubts about whether or not they would ever be able to live "normal" lives after such horrible events, miraculously, almost everything I have heard about them has been positive and encouraging. I know they were all placed in great situations that afforded them the chance for futures that were hopeful and free from the horrors of their early years. Some of them have graduated from college, and others have entered the military. One of them is a commercial pilot.

I don't measure success by money or accomplishments—just the fact that God spared their lives is the most incredible success story imaginable. These children were valuable and precious just as they were, but God wasn't done rescuing them. He also added to each of their lives additional blessings. Have their lives been perfect? Far from it. Did the good that has happened to them erase all the bad? No—the tragedy that remains is just as real as it ever was.

But what should have ended in complete disaster was instead turned into an almost unbelievable story of redemption. Believe it. I was there when it happened. God never gave up on them, and they never gave up either, even when it seemed like they should.

GOD NEVER GAVE UP ON THEM, AND THEY NEVER GAVE UP EITHER, EVEN WHEN IT SEEMED LIKE THEY SHOULD.

Prayers with Soldiers and Letters from Assassins

On one memorable trip, our plane landed in a desert where there was no runway and nothing around for miles. We were supposed to meet our translators and the team with vehicles to help us transport our supplies inland, but they hadn't shown up yet. We were stranded in the middle of a desert until they got there, so we began offloading the supplies while we waited. This load consisted not only of food and water, but also of pots and pans, oil, water cans, dairy cans, and more.

After a few hours, trucks appeared on the distant horizon heading our direction—but as they got closer, it became apparent that they were not our transports. They were a military militia, and once again, we were surrounded by a group of guys with guns. We didn't know if they were good guys from the south or bad guys from the north. Either way, there was no guarantee that this was going to go well for us. It turned out they were from the south, but the man in charge informed us that they were confiscating all of our supplies. He said that his men had nothing, so he had no choice but to take what he needed for his militia.

It seems crazy, but some kind of righteous indignation overtook us. "There's no way in hell you're taking our food!" I said, inching closer to him as I spoke. He didn't flinch, which should have served as a warning sign, but I wasn't paying attention.

He didn't respond kindly to my tone, and an argument ensued between us. Though it didn't deter me in the moment, I do remember thinking that this may have been one of the dumbest things I had ever done. We were in the middle of nowhere, and all these guys had to do was pull a few triggers and no one would ever find us or know what happened to us. Then I said what I should have said from the beginning. "Look, these supplies are for the people that God sent us to help, and He gave us the money to help them. That's why we're here, and that's why we can't let you take this stuff. The people of Sudan need it."

A new expression came across the commander's face. It was as if his eyes had been opened by Someone other than us—and from that moment forward, we had incredible favor with him.

"What you're wanting to do is really good," he said, "and I know where some people are who need it. We'll help you. My men will carry the food and supplies to the camp so that you can give it the people there." You may notice a theme throughout these stories, but I hope that you aren't numbed by what appears to be redundancy. It is not—every single time something like this happened, it was nothing less than miraculous. We could have easily been shot and killed, but instead, those who could have been our enemies helped us with God's mission instead. You will hear more of these kinds of stories ahead, but I hope they will never cease to amaze, as they do for me to this day.

We went with the soldiers, but since we were far removed from our original trip plan, we had nowhere to stay. The commander invited us to spend the night in their camp. We always carry tents, so we pitched them next to the soldiers.

Even if you've only been camping with your family, you know that there is something about sharing a campsite with someone that really bonds you to one another, especially after a long day of working together. We felt a real connection with these guys, most of whom were just boys who had no choice but to fight to survive amid a war they didn't start. They had each lost so much.

We talked into the night and eventually went to sleep. The next morning, over breakfast, the commander said, "Tonight we go into battle against the government forces. Would you pray with our soldiers before we go into battle?" His request was a first for me. Like so many trips, this was not at all what we had planned—yet we could tell God was in it.

"We'd be honored to pray for your soldiers," I replied. I was thinking that we would pray for them right there in the camp, but the commander never opened up the opportunity to do so. We waited all day to pray for them, but the time never came. Late in the afternoon, one of the soldiers approached us and asked if we were ready to go.

"Go where?" I asked.

"Go to pray," he replied.

"Oh."

So the two us left the camp and began following the soldier to parts unknown. We walked for over half an hour, until the camp was far behind us. I finally asked him again, "Where are we going?"

"I'm taking you to pray for the soldiers on the battlefront where the fighting is going to happen tonight."

"Oh," I replied again, but this "oh" sounded different. I was trying not to sound surprised or scared, but I doubt I succeeded. After three hours of walking, we finally reached the place where our campmates were preparing to defend their homeland against the GOS army. The soldiers stood in formation as if they were going to be inspected by a superior officer. Instead, they got us. I remember thinking, *Why am I even here? They need a bishop or somebody like that.*

Despite my insecurities, we began praying for them. I don't even remember what we prayed, but we walked up and down the lines of their formation and prayed over as many soldiers as we could—certainly over every line. There were several thousand of them. When we finished, the commander said, "Okay, you need to get out of here because it's going to get dangerous soon." He sent one soldier with us to keep us from getting lost, and we walked the three hours back to camp.

As darkness fell, we began seeing flashes of light from the distant gunfire and explosions. We could hear and feel the reverberations of the bombs going off. I don't have a military background, but it seemed to be a huge battle that lasted all night. We didn't sleep a wink—after all, our new friends were caught in the fray.

About five o'clock the next morning, the sounds of battle had mostly ceased and some of the soldiers began streaming back into the camp. Soon more followed and the camp began to fill up with soldiers, which we took as a good sign. Many of them even had smiles on their faces. Eventually, the commander showed up. Like the rest, he was covered in dirt, sweat, and soot, but he was alive, and he was also smiling. He approached us, and the way he addressed us seemed like something out of a movie.

"We were outgunned and outmanned. They had bombs and artillery. All we had were guns and a few RPGs. We should have been wiped out. But because you prayed for us, we fought all night and didn't lose a single man. Because of God, we won the battle!" This commander gave Jesus the credit for their protection and victory. We will never know what things God did in the hearts of those soldiers who, perhaps for the first time, discovered that they were heard and valued by the Creator who cared enough to send someone to pray for them.

As we were waiting for our airplane to pick us up, the commander received reports of two GOS helicopter gunships in the area, making it dangerous for our plane to land. We prayed like crazy. Later that day, the plane was finally able to land and pick us up. God continued to keep us hidden under the shadow of His wings. Psalm 91 seems appropriate to apply to our situation: "He will cover you with his feathers. He will shelter you with his wings. His faithful promises are your armor and protection. Do not be afraid of the terrors of the night, nor the arrow that flies in the day" (verses 4-5).

And lest we forget, all of this happened because our transport never showed up in the desert.

In a 2004 letter from an official of the Presbyterian Church of Sudan (PCOS) requesting more relief and aid (included in the photo section with his name redacted for security purposes), a certain soldier who had defected revealed that there had been a serious threat to our lives. They indeed knew what we were doing and, in his words, ". . . your blood and that of your team was supposed to be in the soil of Sudan."

It is crazy that our blood never entered the soil of Sudan. On one occasion, our plane had landed to pick us up when an Antonov bomber flew overhead, ready to drop its payload. Our pilot began taking off—the only problem was, not all of us were on board yet. We began running after the plane down the airstrip and were pulled onboard before the plane gained enough speed to take off.

Another time, we were sleeping in our tents and the GOS tried to bomb us, but they hit an adjacent village instead. We encountered the survivors from the village the next morning—it was a horrible situation, and to this day, I have mixed feelings about what happened. I was no more valuable than those people who lost their lives. There is nothing fruitful to be found down the path of trying to make sense of the senseless violence and destruction we have witnessed. There is no answer to be found that will satisfy.

For me, it all comes down not to understanding, but to the fact that none of this is what God originally intended for humankind. Genesis makes this clear—everything was created to be good, and we were invited not to go down this path and pattern of death. But we insisted on defining good and evil for ourselves rather than trusting in God's love and ways for us. Adam and Eve weren't the only ones who rebelled—we've all done the same ever since.

This is not meant to be a neat summation of the cause of human suffering in the world; rather, it is meant to lead us away from neat summations altogether. I don't know why everything happens the way it does—many events have traumatized me so deeply that I couldn't speak for weeks on end. But I know that this was not what God wanted for us. More importantly, I know that through Christ, God didn't stay away from the pain and suffering, but instead has joined us in it. He is near to the brokenhearted. He knows what it feels like to be tortured and to die. He cares for the little ones and is affectionate towards the elderly who feel they have been forgotten.

"Why" gets us nowhere. Someday, we may know. In the meantime, we're not able to fully understand or process all that happens. But despite all the mysteries of the universe yet unrevealed, God has gone to great lengths to completely end any mystery that remains about how He feels about us! From Genesis to Revelation, His is a message of love and affection for His creation—and a miraculous invitation to adoption as

His children through Christ. There is no suffering that I have seen that God hasn't felt and that Christ isn't in the process of redeeming. That brings me hope when none seems possible to find.

Many times I should have been killed, but God wasn't ready for me to die. I may still be killed someday while doing what God had called me to do. If that ever happens, it does not diminish God's faithfulness or His grace towards me, not even a little bit. Billions of other people throughout history have suffered and died for the cause of Christ. Like me, they all lived and died in His grace.

I CAN DARE TO PURSUE INCREDIBLE AND IMPOSSIBLE THINGS BECAUSE AS LONG AS HE DESIRES ME TO BE HERE, I CAN'T FULLY FAIL.

When I go, peacefully or otherwise, it will simply mean that it is my time and that I have completed the purposes God has for me on earth. As it is said of David in Scripture, ". . . after David had done the will of God in his own generation, he died" (Acts 13:36). All these instances of divine protection simply meant that I had not yet done the full will of God in my own generation. Who knows when that will happen. But I have found a higher courage in knowing that, just like the disappearing billboard stated,

I can dare to pursue incredible and impossible things because as long as He desires me to be here, I can't fully fail. Even when I fail temporarily, God will make His purposes succeed. In this way, my weakness truly is His strength.

The civil war in Sudan was actually a continuation of the first civil war that raged from 1955 to 1972. The violence reemerged in 1983, and the two sides waged war all the way to 2005. Theirs was a history of unspeakable atrocity—and if God is near to those who suffer and are in need, then I know why we felt so drawn there. God was very present in Sudan, which meant we needed to be there too.

On January 9, 2005, the Government of Sudan and the SPLA signed the Comprehensive Peace Agreement, which ended the civil war. The agreement also called for the official creation of South Sudan in 2011, six years after the war ended. When we first started working in Sudan, most relief agencies were afraid to be there because of the civil war. It was also very common for foreigners to "disappear." We were even asked by several organizations why were we going when everyone else was leaving.

Their question held the answer: we went *because* everyone else had left.

As the war came to an end, many of our efforts in Sudan began to shift to other areas of dire need in the world, though certainly there was still much to do in Sudan. With the violence decreasing, other relief organizations and the United

Nations would be able to enter the areas that they had once been warned to avoid. We were very grateful that God was opening the door for more help from others for a people we had come to love so very deeply.

Statistics would not do any justice to what God did during the five years or so that we ventured into the darkest and neediest places of Sudan. All told, hundreds of thousands of pounds of food and supplies were delivered. Medical aid was dispensed. The plight of the slave was brought to light, and in many cases those slaves, many of them children, were set free.

The true value was joining real people in their suffering and watching God use people like us—people who had no earthly business being there in the first place—to make a heavenly difference in a world that seemed like hell.

FIVE

Warlords, Children, and Heroes

Afghanistan and Pakistan

As I've already briefly shared, during our time in Sudan, we were simultaneously working in other parts of the world—one of which was a nation brutally hit by war and destruction on an indescribable scale: Afghanistan. About nine months before the attacks of 9/11, I was working in Sudan when God spoke to me about going to Afghanistan.

You also already know that our first trip there found us surrounded by armed Taliban guards miraculously sent not to hurt us, but to escort us to one of the camps where desperate refugees were freezing and starving. When we arrived at the camp, we assessed the situation and realized that the refugees not only had no food, but they also had no pots or pans—that is, no ability to prepare food even if we brought it to them. We came back the next day with a plan.

We met with the leaders of the camp and explained all that needed to be done to properly distribute food and supplies. A plan in these kinds of situations is very important because when people are exceptionally desperate, getting it wrong can be a recipe for disaster—including violence, rioting, and more death. The leaders agreed to our plan and let us set up our operation in a vacant area where we could park all our trucks and vehicles.

Over the next several days, we ramped up for the distribution process. We prepared individualized bags that contained cooking oil and a few utensils, along with rice and beans. Finally we were able to begin distributing food and supplies to the people who needed it the most. One of our core values is to be present whenever possible to ensure that help is being offered to the right people. These were the right people.

One day, one of the main Taliban leaders said, "We want to honor you at a meal tonight." I wondered where they would find the food for such a meal, but sure enough, I soon found myself with a bunch of soldiers in their commander's quarters. They put a leather rug on the floor and spread plates with food across it. We all sat down, and everyone began reaching in and partaking of the meal together. We even took a picture together around the makeshift table (see photo section).

We had been running like madmen through all the necessary stages of planning and distribution, but this moment caused me to come back to myself. I breathed for the first time in weeks. As I did, God whispered to my heart, "Did I not tell you that I would make a table before you in the presence of your enemies?"

His internal whisper filled me with a renewed sense of assurance. I knew that no matter what happened in Afghanistan, we would be safe. I would never have to worry—even though we would experience worrisome events in the coming years. Even if we were to lose our lives, God was present in all of it, and we could trust Him.

That night around that table, our new friends honored us greatly. They knew we were Christians. In fact, to an Afghan, if you're from the West, you're a Christian, whether you really are or not. The fact that our religions have historically viewed one another as enemies did not stop God from connecting us in peace through His work of reaching those most desperately in need. Our work in Afghanistan would last nearly a decade—and this whisper from God about trusting Him in danger would one day be severely tested.

Zorha

The stories of our time in Afghanistan are too many to fully tell, but they don't all revolve around guns and war. We were able to deliver food and supplies to a people we came to adore. The Afghans were some of the kindest and most generous people I ever met, even though their situation was dire.

On our first trip to Kabul, we found a level of devastation almost beyond belief. Nearly every building and structure in the city was leveled—and anything that was left standing was riddled with bullet holes. Even the hotel room where we slept at night had bullet holes in every wall.

There was one part of Kabul where even the Afghans we were working with didn't want to go because it was not safe or secure. Naturally, we felt that this was where God was calling us. We ventured into this slum area to see who might be in need.

We discovered that the elders of the city were forcing refugees coming down from the north to stay in this quarter of the city—like forced segregation. As you can imagine, crime and poverty were out of control, and many people in need were falling through the cracks. These refugees literally had nothing and were huddling together in the freezing cold inside old, bombed-out buildings, some of which were falling down around them. They slept up against half walls, shivering, sick, and starving.

We made our way through the rubble and began meeting these people. We told them that we had come to help them. That's when someone brought us a tiny infant named Zorha. She was eighteen months old but only weighed eleven pounds. The pictures of this precious child are the only way to do justice to her condition (see photo section). She was severely malnourished and only hours from death. She looked like skin and bone on a skeleton—and we knew we had to do something fast if we wanted to save her life.

Zorha's father had been killed, and her mother had been forced to remarry his brother. But unfortunately the brother didn't want Zorha, so she had been given to a very elderly grandmother, who was doing everything in her power to take care of this baby in a bombed-out, freezing war zone where she was barely surviving herself.

With their permission, we rushed Zorha away from the rubble to the only hospital that was still operational in Kabul after all the bombing. The doctors told us that her condition was extremely severe, but they would do their best. We left her there and returned to help the people back in the slums.

We began organizing and distributing enough food, blankets, cooking stoves, and other supplies to help these poor people survive their next day. I cannot overstate how gracious they were to us—so very warm and kind. To Western eyes and perspectives, Afghan culture can seem cold, standoffish, or hard. But when you get them behind closed doors and really connect with them as people, they are some of the most welcoming folks in the world—and they can't do enough to help you. Above all, they treat others with honor.

Let's be clear: God didn't just send me to affect the refugees—He sent them to deeply affect me. I was more honored to meet them than they were to meet me. But God loves us all—that's why He put us together.

Three months later, we received a photo[2] of Zorha, and once again, only the pictures can do it justice. She had gone

2 See photo section.

from a skeleton to exactly what she should have been: a healthy, happy, chunky little baby girl. God had rescued her little life because He valued her so very much.

Zorha's transformation deeply impacted all the people in this slum area. They told us that their own Muslim Afghan brothers had never come to help them. Only the Christians from the West came, and they saved this child's life. We didn't preach at them, but we did continue to share the reason we had come: because Jesus loved them and had sent us to help. The message seemed to resonate with them. One of our core values echoes the expression sometimes attributed to St. Francis of Assisi: preach the gospel at all times, and when necessary, use words. Our actions opened their hearts to the words of our message: "God loves you!"

PREACH THE GOSPEL AT ALL TIMES, AND WHEN NECESSARY, USE WORDS.

From 2001 to 2013, there were countless other children like Zorha whom God honored us with the task of serving. Crisis Aid began to expand in ways we never thought possible. God sent donors and partners who saw what was going on in Sudan and Afghanistan and wanted to join our work, and together, the whole of our efforts was so much greater than the sum of its parts. In 2005 alone, we delivered 526,000 pounds (263 tons) of food to various people in need around the world. We learned new techniques to maximize the relief efforts, such as timing food distribution trips so the meals would last through the most severe part of the winter.

In Afghanistan, we also helped provide training to hundreds of widows, teaching them how to sew. Over time, they produced thousands of heavy blankets that we were able to distribute throughout impoverished areas prior to the onset of winter. We were able to purify approximately 1,400 wells, which prevented cholera outbreaks in some parts of the country. We provided funds to support local schools that educated young girls, which caused their enrollments to triple. We also partnered with other organizations that have the same heart as Crisis Aid so we could reach even more people.

In some ways, our efforts in Afghanistan always come back to one of the first children we ever met: Zorha. She changed all of our lives, but the crazy thing was, we almost didn't get to meet her, or the precious people in the slums where she lived.

Hot Heads and Trigger Fingers

Rewind to our second trip, not long after the United States began bombing Afghanistan. We landed near another un-disclosed border town. Since I often leave out the identities of the people who make up the "we" for security reasons, I will be calling one of my partners in this mission by the name of Robert.

I remember showing up at a hotel in Nairobi to meet Robert and another guy, not having any clue what we were supposed to be doing. They knocked on my door, and the second I met Robert, we both instantly knew that we would be working together for a long time. For years, that's exactly what we did, pooling our resources and connections. Our work together had begun in Sudan, but it didn't end there. Robert was there when I sat up in the middle of the night in Sudan and said, "I think God wants me to go to Afghanistan." After 9/11, I called to tell him I was going, and he said he would meet me there. But true to Robert's nature, he beat me there. We were more than just friends. We were like blood brothers.

Of course, brothers know how to fight with each other as well.

Our second trip took us to a different location than the first. A few weeks earlier, a carload of foreign journalists from reputable media outlets had been pulled out of their vehicle and killed. It was a dangerous situation for Westerners. Only our friend in the Pakistani government knew we were there. We also hired an Afghan translator from the area to assist.

Robert and I spent several days trying to figure out how to get food to the next group of refugees. Everyone knew that there were refugee camps all along the border of Pakistan— the international news organizations were reporting on it left and right. People were starving in Afghanistan, but it seemed like no one was able to get to them to help.

After asking around for a few days, we were told that there was no food available—and also no vehicles available to transport any that might be found. The infuriating part was that we watched huge trucks loaded down with sacks of grain coming and going in the town streets. There was obviously food somewhere, but it was being used for the military, not the refugees. We had lots of cash on us—enough to buy the supplies—but we had no way of accessing them.

The logistical situation was a complete lockdown, with zones being controlled by various military warlords and passage between them virtually impossible without being captured or killed. We began thinking that we might just have to go back home because there was no feasible way to reach the people. This made us very upset—and as the days passed, our irritability only grew. We were tired and stressed.

Somehow, we were able to secure a meeting with one of the commanding generals in charge of the entire Afghan-Pakistani border region. I don't know how it happened, but we were assured that this guy was the one who called the shots—and he agreed to meet with us

We arrived where we were told to go only to find ourselves standing in an alley. Immediately, it felt all wrong. There were soldiers protecting the compound where we were supposed to meet the leader. They stood all around us with AK-47s. This felt familiar, but not in a good way. There were maybe a dozen of them, and they did not seem very happy that we were there.

I know that I've described moments of being afraid, but even in those instances, there is usually some sense of peace—like a grace from God that I can tangibly feel. For whatever reason, that grace was lifted right then. The result was that Robert and I fell apart.

As we waited in the alley for our meeting with the general, it was as if our eyes were opened to the level of danger we were in. We both suddenly saw it and responded with, "What in the world are we doing here?" We realized that we were surrounded, and an argument erupted between us. We had been like brothers for several years, but now we were at each other's throats.

Finally, Robert screamed, "I'm done! I'm leaving!"

"Where do you think you're going to go? Look around you, man! There's no getting out of this!"

The Taliban soldiers just stood there staring at us, probably trying to figure out what in the world we had been smoking. Every single one of them, some who seemed to be as young as twelve or thirteen, had an AK-47 slung over his shoulder. I've never seen so many guns in my entire life. Of course, the United States was still actively bombing the area, so I wasn't exactly the most popular guy in the alley. Their faces said it all.

Finally, the commander was ready to see us. We walked through a door in the alley and onto an outdoor patio. There were three chairs set up inside—one for each of us and one for the general who was sitting across from us. Through the translator, he told us to sit down.

We were now surrounded by guards who were holding their AK-47s in their hands. Throughout my travels, I have learned to pay attention to whether or not a guy with a gun has his finger resting on the trigger. It is the first thing I look for. If their fingers are on the triggers, it's usually a bad sign.

All around us, fingers were on triggers.

As the commander stared at us, we were still whisper fighting back and forth in English like children, trying to come up with some kind of plan to survive this mess.

"You lead!" I said.

"Me? I'm from South Africa! You're a Christian from America!"

"So what?" I shot back.

"So that means if they're going to kill anybody, it's you—I'm not saying anything!" I called him by a name that shouldn't be printed here. You get the gist. The commander was apparently over our bickering, so through the translator, he finally asked, "Why are you here?" I didn't speak Pashtun, but his tone indicated that he felt put out by our presence in the middle of such a pressing time for his people. He had bigger things to worry about, and we were feeling more and more like an inconvenient loose end with each passing minute.

I knew that this would probably be the last conversation I would have in this life, and perhaps that provided me with some clarity. If I was going down, I wanted to do so by the truth of what led me there in the first place. "We are here because we want to help the Afghan people—because God loves them so much. God sees their suffering. He sees the children who are dying. He sees the widows. He sees people freezing in the night. It's breaking His heart, and He told people in America to give us money so we could help you."

The translator finished interpreting to the commander, who sat looking at us with a quiet intensity. The entire fifteen-minute interaction had been incredibly tense, but suddenly, his whole body language changed. He leaned back in his chair and almost began to appear . . . well, relaxed. As soon as he did, I noticed that all of the fingers around us came off of their triggers. The guards were reading his every move.

Then the commander spoke to us in perfect English: "I honor you." That may not seem like a very big deal in Western culture, but we were told that if an Afghan makes that statement to you, it means that his life is now tied to yours. From that point forward, if anything were to happen to us, he would be honor bound to respond in equal measure. If someone killed us, he was honor bound to kill them. He continued, "I honor you because I know that your God has sent you because you have spoken the truth to me."

One of my first thoughts was, *Holy Lord! Why didn't You tell us that he could speak English! We could have said the wrong thing and been killed on the spot!*

"What do you need?" he continued.

We told him that we needed food and trucks to transport it—and we wanted to know where the area of greatest need was so we could go where no one else was willing or able to go.

He told us about a village in the foothills of the border "where your country is bombing." There were more than five thousand people there who had not had any food for several weeks and were in very bad shape. The problem wasn't just what was happening, but also where they were. They were located three zones away, and each zone was controlled by different factions and warlords. If we were to move from one zone to the next without permission, they would kill us on the spot—especially since we looked and sounded like—well, us.

There may have been only one guy in the entire region who had the clout to get us safe access across these zones, and we were sitting with him.

"I will get you the trucks," he said. "And I will get you the food, if you can pay for it."

"We can pay for it," we replied.

"I'm also going to give you my personal bodyguard. My father-in-law will head up your security team. You will be watched over twenty-four hours a day while you're in my country. No harm will come to you." Everyone knew that this father-in-law represented the commander, so coming against one of them was coming against the other. With that, our meeting ended and we emerged alive. Later we were able to laugh about the argument, but the time for laughing was still a long way off.

After we spent a day or two shoring up our supplies and logistical arrangements with his men, we were driven safely across the various war zones and into the mountainside village. The people had heard we were coming and were waiting for us. The soldiers helped us offload and distribute the food to the people. We told them that God loved the Afghans, and that was why we were there. They listened and received our message with gratitude. There was no hostility at all.

There was no place for us to stay in the village, and our security team did not feel that they could keep us safe from danger or the elements—after all, the temperatures plummeted at nighttime. So the father-in-law said that they would drive us back to the city. Driving through these areas at night was literally inviting death. However, with our new friends we never came under fire.

God's grace had brought us into their honor. We made it out alive, but that wasn't the case for everyone who served God in the causes of justice, compassion, and aid in Afghanistan.

Heroes

Back in the first chapter, I talked about my friend named Shahbaz, who was an official in the Pakistani government and who assisted us over the years. He was one of the only Christians in national leadership—and he was a very close friend of mine.

Once we had been working in the country for some time doing relief work, we began meeting local Afghan Christians who expressed the need for ministry resources and training in their own language. But they had no means of supporting themselves in ministry. We carefully began walking down the path of meeting with these underground church leaders, knowing that theirs was a dangerous and courageous faith walk.

With Shahbaz's assistance, we began to launch a plan to help these ministry leaders. We adopted a two-year curriculum that led to an associate's degree in Biblical studies. It was known for being very biblically sound and for being translated into dozens of languages around the world. However, it had never been translated into Pashtun, the predominant language in the region. The leaders of the organization that had created the curriculum, International School of Ministry (ISOM), were very excited when we contacted them about the need for this translation. Soon, it became a shared project with ISOM to provide the materials to Shahbaz, who agreed to help with the translation.

Shahbaz was very well known in the region. As one of the only outspoken Christians in the Pakistani government, he was a human rights advocate who spoke out against violence, including the persecution of Christians. He also spoke out against Sharia law and advocated for the marginalized and the poor in the Middle East. I would like to say that we became first-time instant best friends, but the truth is, the first time I met him, I wanted to kill him. He showed up eight hours late to meet us and still claimed he was on time. However, we became second-time instant best friends, which I guess proves that first impressions can't always be trusted.

Shahbaz and I always kept a bit of banter going on between us. He was greatly concerned about us working in Sudan because he thought it was too dangerous. I thought that was hilarious, since he was an evangelical Christian working in the Pakistani government. He would always say that I was going to be the first one of us to get killed, and I would say that he would be the first one. Writing it down now, I see exactly how weird that might sound to a "normal" person, but out on the front lines, it was easier to have a laugh in the middle of the danger than to sit around dwelling on the heavy parts of it all day long. We had to trust God either way, so we tried to have some fun in the meantime. Only God's peace allowed this.

Shahbaz began helping us with the translation, but with all of his other duties, it proved to be just a bit too much for him to handle. We found another Pakistani pastor who agreed to work on completing the translation for the entire three trimesters. We gave him the English materials, and he translated them into audio materials recorded in Pashtun. It would ultimately become a printed course, but we didn't have time to wait for that lengthy publishing process. Instead, we simply recorded the translations into an audio format and sent them to ISOM, who in turn would master the tracks to maximize their audio quality and send the master tapes back to us so we could duplicate them as needed.

We began distributing the tapes and training ministers, which was an incredible process. God raised up many amazing people who were willing to take the risk of seeking a ministry education for the purpose of reaching others for Christ. The program took off and grew, lasting for several years. Our process included training and then sending people into various areas of Afghanistan as evangelists (but we just called them our "friends") to share the gospel and help establish underground churches. They would go in for three weeks at a time, then return to us to rest, debrief, continue training, and go back in. All told, we sent out twenty-one friends.

Afghans began giving their lives to Christ left and right. People don't realize how much 9/11 did for the cause of the gospel in that area. Most Afghans we met were against what happened. People would approach us and tell us that what happened was not at all a reflection of their Islam, which they insisted called for peace and not for acts of murder or terror. Again, I love the graciousness and gentleness of the Afghan people.

One of our main friends was an amazing man named Babar. He was a pastor in Pakistan who lived about fifty miles from the border and helped us organize and distribute information to the friends we were sending out. One day, he called me with some bad news. One of our friends was home in his village when the Taliban came to his house and pulled him and his family out into the middle of the square. They gathered the entire village around and said, "This man has converted to Christianity, and he's trying to get other Afghans to do the same. This is what we will do to anyone who does what he has done." They slit his throat right there in front of his wife and two small children—he bled out and died at their feet.

I couldn't believe my ears. It was not as if we had never thought of these possibilities, but I couldn't believe it was actually happening to one of our friends. I would meet with each of our friends two or three times a year. In our meeting, I would always ask the question, "What happens if you're caught?" Every one of them replied that they would most likely be killed.

"And what about your families?" I would ask.

"They could possibly be killed too."

Every one of them knew the price they might have to pay, yet they were willing to do it. They would, however, often ask me what we would do for their families if they were killed and their families survived. It was complicated due to the nature of our arrangement, so I could never promise anything specific. But I did promise that we would do everything in our power to help in any way possible. My word to try was all I could offer.

Three days later, Babar called me again. We had lost another one. This time, it was our friend Wadak. He was an Afghan who was very funny and who loved me dearly. He often used to say, "Pat, anytime you come to my country, you will always be safe because I will always take the bullet that's meant for you."

Wadak had gone to the village of the first martyr to offer comfort and assistance to his family. When he left their home, two guys walked up to him on the street, put a gun to his chest, and said, "We know all about what you're doing." Then they pulled the trigger and murdered him in broad daylight, leaving his body there in the street.

This seemed like the lowest point, but things went from bad to worse.

At this time, I was still coming back and forth to my advertising job. A few days after Wadak's death, I was meeting with some clients in our conference room when my phone rang. It was Shahbaz, who never called me at that time of day. There were about nine people in the room at the time, so I stepped out and took the call.

Shahbaz was shaken. He said that Babar and Daniyal, two of our main leaders of the friends, had been kidnapped at gunpoint. No one had heard from them in two days. My heart sank.

Over the next several days, we tried to wrap our heads around what was happening. We discovered that the enemy had not only kidnapped them, but they had also confiscated all of the ISOM materials, computers, equipment, and tapes. Babar had been helping us to store and manage the information, but our system lacked the best security protocols or encryption.

Several days later, Babar and Daniyal were found handcuffed together on the side of the road. Their noses and ears had been cut off, and they had each been shot more than twenty times. We were devastated for their families—and for the implications of what this might mean for the rest of the Afghan Christians whom we had trained and who were being supported on a monthly basis. Our friend network had grown to twenty-one, but that number was quickly decreasing.

Within six months, nine of our friends had lost their lives.

When Shahbaz told me about Daniyal and Babar, I told him that I was going to drop everything and try to get there. "Can you hold off on their funerals for a few days?" I asked.

"No, Pat, we can't do that," Shahbaz replied.

I had to keep my word, but it seemed like everything was against me. My visa into Pakistan had expired several months earlier. I had reapplied as always, but this time, they were not approving it as usual. Shahbaz found out through some of his sources that I had been blacklisted because of our work with the Christians.

We found a workaround. I secured a second US passport that made it through their screening process undetected. By the time Shahbaz called to tell me about Babar and Daniyal, I already had my new visa approved, so as quickly as I could secure a flight, I jumped on a plane on my way to Islamabad.

I first flew from St. Louis to Chicago for a layover. As I waited, the gravity of the whole situation fell on me like a ton of bricks. It was one of the most dangerous scenarios imaginable. I remember standing in the corner of the airport and feeling completely alone, contemplating the idea of not going. I had a wife and kids, and if I went, I wasn't sure that I would ever make it back home. No one would fault me for not going.

GOD ALREADY KNEW WHAT I WAS GOING TO DO, BUT HE WANTED ME TO FACE WHETHER OR NOT I WOULD TRUST IN THE FAITH HE HAD PROVIDED.

Brother Andrew once told me that God could never trust my faith until He tested my faith. God already knew what

I was going to do, but He wanted me to face whether or not I would trust in the faith He had provided. In that moment in Chicago, a war was raging inside me in a way I had never before experienced. I felt led to call a certain friend, and we prayed together. Her words and prayers reminded me that God was with me and equipped me with new courage. Ultimately, I boarded the next plane to London on my way to Islamabad.

After I landed, I called Shahbaz from the airport. He had been doing some clandestine digging to determine the extent of our security breach. It had started with the Pakistani ISI, which is like our CIA. They had broken our network security and hacked our information, passing it along to the Taliban. That was how they began picking off our evangelists in the first place—and then, of course, once they killed Babar, they found the mother lode of information from the computers. They knew everything from my name and address to the bank account information we had been using to fund the program and support our friends in ministry.

Oh, and one more thing: they had put out a contract on my life—the second one that I know of.

"Pat, you can't come into the city!" Shahbaz was insistent that it was too dangerous.

"But I gave my word!"

"It's too dangerous! You're not good to anyone dead!"

"I don't care! What is it going to say to the rest of our friends if I don't keep my word to be here for them?"

"Fine," Shahbaz relented, "but you must go straight to your hotel and nowhere else." I agreed and made it to my hotel late that night. Shahbaz had his own underground contacts and networks all over the country, so by the time I walked into the hotel lobby about midnight, a husband and wife came up to meet me. I knew they were from Shahbaz.

They didn't want to come up to my room, so I went up, dropped off my stuff, and came back down to meet with them in the lobby. We talked for about thirty minutes. The entire time we interacted, their eyes were moving all around the room, watching every exit. There were other undercover agents outside the doors. The whole thing was very unnerving because I was being watched, possibly by more than one group, and one set of eyes on me was not at all friendly.

Shahbaz was afraid that I would be kidnapped, but I was afraid of breaking my promise to the families of our friends. The next morning, Shahbaz picked me up and we left the hotel and bounced all around the city for a few hours, almost as if we were trying to lose anyone who might be following us. He finally took me to a small hotel where he knew the owner.

He told me that every exit of the first hotel had been watched all night by his people. They were afraid that the ISI would come to my room and take me hostage, so if that were to happen, his contacts would have followed us to know where I had been taken. By God's grace and according to His will, it never happened, and I saw the light of the next day.

I spent a few days there, and Shahbaz let all the friends and their families know where I was, but none of them would come see me. This was not to preserve their safety; they were trying to preserve mine. They did send word, however, that it meant the world that I had come, as I promised I would. We began offering support to the widows and families the best that we could.

Sadly, since our entire network was compromised, we had to shut everything down. Many of the remaining friends and their families moved to other parts of the country for their safety, so we lost contact with them, though we know that they took the message of Christ with them. This was the beginning of the end of our time in Afghanistan.

Some eight years later, I was speaking with a man who told me that the materials we had created were still being used with great effectiveness in some parts of the country, so our work wasn't in vain. One cannot overstate the kinds of risks that these heroes were willing to take to live out their faith and share the hope of Jesus with others. I remember being in an underground church meeting in a house, just sitting in a room with some Afghan friends after we had walked through a back alley to get there. It was late at night so as not to arouse any suspicion, and we were sitting on the floor, just talking and praying together.

All of a sudden, there was a knock at the door. Every single one of us felt a jolt of almost crippling anxiety because everyone who knew about the meeting was already there. We expected the next sound to be the door being kicked in or grenades flying through the windows. My heart stopped. When we finally opened the door, it was another believer who had heard there was a meeting with some believers from the West.

This has happened to me a few times, but this scenario happens for believers in that part of the world every day. A crazy story for me is an everyday occurrence for them. They need our prayers and our support.

The Best of Us . . . The Worst of Events

On March 2, 2011, I was in Denver to interview a development person about fundraising. Our meeting was in a little café breakfast joint, and the news was playing on a TV in the background. I wasn't really paying attention to it.

That is, until CNN flashed a picture of Shahbaz across the screen. I did a double take, but sure enough, it was him. He had been sitting in standstill traffic in Islamabad at about 7:30 in the morning when some guys pulled him out of his car and shot him twenty-five times right there in the street. Shahbaz was dead.

We had been so close. He had stayed at my house. He had worked behind the scenes to help many people in need. He had guarded my life on many occasions. Now he was gone— and it rocked me to my very core.

Honestly, to this day, it still does. My shock and grief notwithstanding, at first, I was surprised that his death made international headlines. If I were to die, no one in the world would really be the wiser besides a few friends and family. Yet over the days that followed, I discovered that Shahbaz was much more influential than he had ever let on. He was humble.

I was shocked to see on the news and in newspapers that multiple former US presidents released statements about his death, including President George W. Bush and President Bill Clinton. I also read statements from the Chancellor of Germany, the President of France, and the Prime Minister of the UK. They all condemned his assassination, extolling all the positive things Shahbaz had done for humanitarian purposes.

I found out that the US State Department used to regularly fly him to the States every year for a full week of meetings. During that time, he would meet with members of Congress, senators, and the president, discussing geopolitical and humanitarian issues in the Middle East and what could be done to help those most in need. The whole time, Shahbaz had been a major player on the global stage, but he kept it below the radar with me. My surprise soon subsided when I put it all together—anyone who was that good of a friend and that faithful to God was no doubt capable of being used by God to affect change on a global scale.

The Pakistani government covered up the murder, and to this day, no one has ever been prosecuted.

The death of nine of our friends had severely affected our efforts, but Shahbaz's death marked the end of our ability to effectively work in Afghanistan. When I look back at the pictures, as I hope you will do as well, my heart is filled with fond memories of our time there—and many painful ones as well. Though it ended with such heartache, I still have no doubt that God sent us there, and for a decade He met needs that defied adequate description in unimaginable ways.

John the Baptist also experienced moments of heartache and confusion—moments when what he believed and what he had done ran headlong into unexpected tragedy. He started out as the most famous preacher around, but then quickly and wholeheartedly pointed people to Jesus instead, knowing that his entire purpose in ministry was to prepare people's hearts to follow someone other than himself. Yet as a little time passed, John found himself not traveling with Jesus and the rest of his disciples. Instead, he found himself languishing in a prison for political reasons—and certainly not for any crimes he had committed.

In that moment, he wasn't sure how to reconcile it all. He decided to reach out and seek wisdom from the One he had directed everyone else to follow. Jesus had the power to heal sick people, give the blind their sight, raise the dead, and most definitely, snap His fingers and release John the Baptist—His cousin and most loyal and selfless follower—from prison. It seemed like a fairly logical sequence for any of us looking in from the outside. Why was Jesus not helping His buddy John?

Jesus' response to John brings me such comfort when I think about my nine friends, their families, and Shahbaz: "Then he told John's disciples, 'Go back to John and tell him what you have seen and heard—the blind see, the lame walk, those with leprosy are cured, the deaf hear, the dead are raised to life, and the Good News is being preached to the poor.' And he added, 'God blesses those who do not fall away because of me'" (Luke 7:22-23).

Shortly thereafter, John would be beheaded in prison. Jesus never came to physically rescue him. Even so, John's life was far from wasted. He had served the purposes of God and helped many people experience healing and life through their interactions with Christ. There is no doubt that John was discouraged and doubting, but Jesus reminded him not to let his faith fall by the wayside just because the outcomes were not as he had predicted or desired.

My friends who lost their lives in our collective operations in Afghanistan may have died in seemingly senseless ways, but they did not die in vain. While they lived, lives were changed as the Good News was delivered to the poorest of the poor— the news that God sees them in their need and sent His own Son, who sent us to care for those needs. It did not end as we wanted, but any earthly ending is only temporary. The Good News continues forward, and their lives continue forever in a place where violence can never again reach them.

Presbyterian Church of The Sudan

الكنيسة المشيخية السودانية

P.O. Box
Nairobi, Kenya.
Tel:
Fax:
E mail: pcos

Headquarter
Leer-South Sudan

Western Upper Nile Presbytery

Mr Pat Bradley
ICA

24 November 2004

Dear Sir

On behalf of the Presbyterian Church of Sudan (PCOS) and the Sudanese people of the Western Upper Nile (WUN), we would like to express our sincere appreciation for all your efforts and assistance in recent years as you stood with us during difficult times of war. Your organisation cared and looked after our people during times when our area was NO GO for other NGO's and the UN. You took great risks to be with us and also experienced some of the attacks that we face on a daily basis, for this we are most grateful to you.

Recently at a meeting in Nairobi, a commander who defected from the Government of Sudan stated that they knew you and your work and what you were doing in the WUN for our people, he also stated that your blood and of your team was supposed to be in the soil of Sudan.

Sudan continues to face great difficulties with little NGO assistance in most parts of WUN and Darfur, attacks still take place and people continue to suffer. NGO organizations are still not prepared to take the risk to reach our area and this is why we are appealing to you and your organization for help. Our people desperately need help as we are in the dry season with no crops or reserves, our children do not receive education as there are no schools, we have no health clinics and people die from simple diseases, please Mr Pat, we seek your help.

The Sudanese people value your continued support and friendship and would like to say a big thank you.

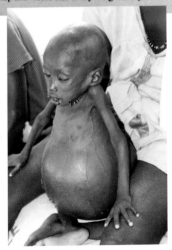

Upper Photo:
Letter from Presbyterian
Church of Sudan.
Story on Page 111.

Bottom Photo:
Sudanese child with cancer.
Story on Page 87.

Before picture of Zorha.

After picture of Zorha.
Story on Page 120.

A table in the presence of your enemies. Story on Page 118.

A supply distribution site in the middle of nowhere.

Afghan girl.

Wadak. Story on Page 135.

Some of the recipients of an Afghan distribution.

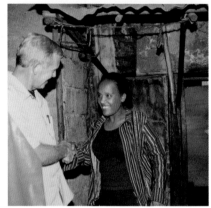

Some of the girls that were rescued from the red light district.

One of the streets in the red light district.

Access to clean water is life-changing for so many.

Upper Photo:
Hiwot at her graduation in December 2020.

Bottom Photo:
Hiwot with severe series of tumors.
Story on Page 182.

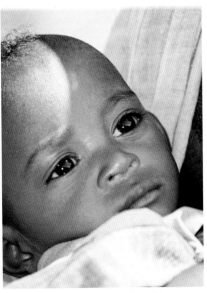

Esther at 1 week old.
Story on Page 155.

Esther at 3 months old.

Before picture of Sofiya.

Sofiya after 21 months.

Tigist on the day we found her.

Tigist and her older brother.

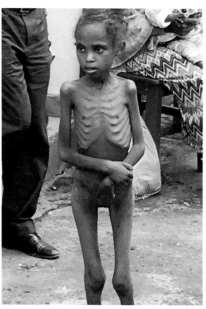

Zuri in October 2018.

Zuri in May 2019.

Metawork died shortly after this photo was taken.

Asha tragically died soon after this photo was taken.
Story on Page 170.

Susan with one of the girls rescued from the red light district.
She now owns her own business.

Pat and Sue stood as the parents for this young lady
who was rescued from the red light district.

A girl in the red light district.

Village in Cambodia.
Story on Page 214.

Inside a room in the red light district.

Graduation ceremony at Mercy Chapel.

Orphanage that was destroyed by an earthquake in Haiti.

U.S. Marines unloading food after the Haiti earthquake.

A room in the red light district.

Marine helicopter loaded for food distribution. Story on Page 240.

Pat with one of the graduates.

Mercy Chapel graduate.

All smiles on graduation day.

Ready to start a new life
out of the red light district.

Pat holding Lemlem.
Story on Page 179.

Lemlem after her first surgery.

Melasech is proof of the power of one yes.
Story on Page 196.

Susan and Pat celebrating with several of their friends.

Girls from our children's home.

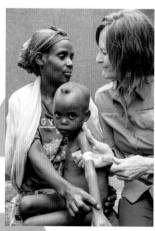

Susan comforts a mother.

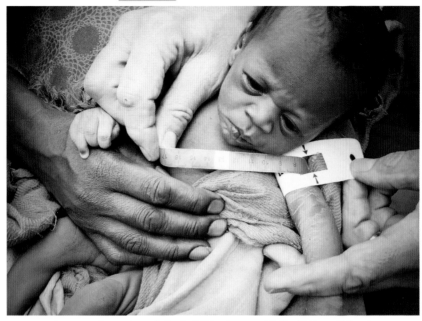

A severely malnourished child who would die if they did not
get the help our generous donors make possible.

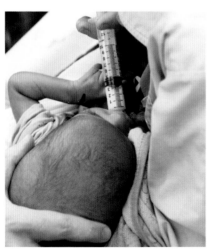

A malnourished baby being fed
via a syringe.

A Mercy Chapel student learns
the art of hair dressing.

SIX

Post-It Notes and Promises

East Africa

I can't remember what I had for breakfast that day or what was on my work calendar, but I will never forget the headline that I read on my computer. "14 million East Africans at Risk of Death by Starvation." To be clear, this headline named the country in East Africa where this horrific reality was daily unfolding, but for the sake of our ongoing work there, we will just call it East Africa.

It was 2003, and our work in both Sudan and Afghanistan was ongoing, as was my job as a full-time businessman. With all the logistics, planning, and lists of things to do swirling in my mind, this headline suddenly brought all the mess to a mental standstill. Instantaneously, I recognized God's whisper, which by this time was becoming more familiar

"Go."

I began making some phone calls, and thirty days later, I landed in the nation's capital city with nothing to go on but a phone number on a yellow Post-It note. All my calls had produced nothing in terms of a network of local contacts or ideas of what we could possibly do to help the situation. It was frustrating, but I knew that God had said to go, and I had already had enough experiences in Sudan and Afghanistan to understand that God impressions are worth following, even when you don't know exactly where you are going.

When I got off the plane, I dialed the phone number, and it turned out to be a large church organization in the country that had its own development wing—this was the direct number to the guy in charge. Before we knew it, he set up a six-day trip for us into the bush of East Africa, going village to village to see what was going on so we could begin making plans to help.

You already know many of the horrors of what I had seen in Sudan and Afghanistan, but specifically concerning starvation, what I saw in East Africa was unlike anything I'd ever witnessed. Men, women, and children were literally dying because they had no food whatsoever. Later, when I spoke with a government official and a representative from the UN, I was told that if a feeding program was not implemented immediately, eighty to ninety percent of the babies in these areas would die in the next two to four weeks—and in many cases, everyone present would most likely be dead within the next two months. This was happening on a mass scale all around the region.

How could this be? Was this region just overpopulated and stuck in poverty where they could not or would not work to provide for their families? No, it was much more complicated and tragic, though many Westerners tend to jump to simpler conclusions simply because it is hard to understand the depths of what is happening in other parts of the world.

The scope of these problems was beginning to widen for me.

I learned that East Africa had been struck by severe drought conditions for a very long time—six years or so. It was called the green drought. When it did rain, it often fell fast and hard, completely flooding farmland not able to sustain even mild floods. Instead of feast or famine, the rain situation was flood or famine—and both led to famine.

The people living in these conditions were far from lazy. They planted every available inch of ground that might possibly sustain crops, but unfortunately, those areas were limited. Some places were impossible for planting, especially on the sides of mountains that sloped more than seventy degrees in places. They also lacked modern farm equipment, which meant that all the farming had to be done with oxen pulling plows. In the midst of the famine, many of them had to sell their oxen to buy food, or their oxen died from a lack of food and water. This was the land of the malnourished cows.

The cycle of poverty and starvation seemingly had no hope of ending. At times, we drove for more than three hours past vast fields planted with corn, as much as one might see in the American Midwest. But every stalk of corn had died. Despite their best efforts, the ground and the sky were completely unforgiving. The toll had now been taken—multiple years without consistent rain had dried up everything in sight. Their crops died, along with their hope.

In one of the most remote areas, about five thousand families were living in these conditions. Food distribution efforts by humanitarian groups were not reaching them this far out. Mothers were trying to make meals from the roots of Enset trees (also known as false banana trees), sometimes being forced to mix in dirt just to fill their children's bellies. This caused terrible sickness, but survival sometimes requires extreme actions. Some people were walking more than four hours (one way) in an effort to hire themselves out just to earn enough to feed their families for one day. For most, if they earned fifty cents to one dollar, it was a good day. Unfortunately, there were not many good days to be had.

Water was also a serious problem. People were getting their drinking water from any puddles that remained after small, quick rains. Many of the rivers and wells had dried up. People had no choice but to walk several hours to retrieve water from muddy, unsanitary rivers.

On the sixth day of our trip, we came up a hill to a village where about 250 women were just sitting with their children. Many of them had two or three children, and every single child in that village was obviously severely malnourished. Do not take these words as an exaggeration—I will explain more in the pages ahead, but for now, "severely malnourished" means that 100 percent of the time, a child will die if he or she doesn't get help soon. The elders came out to meet us, sharing more of their stories and talking about what they needed.

After six days, I had seen enough to know exactly what we had to do. I told them that we needed to erect a therapeutic feeding center, or TFC, as soon as possible. I had learned that a TFC would cost about $100,000 to construct and furnish. I didn't tell them how much it cost—they were paying the ultimate cost already. They begged us to do something because things were getting worse by the day.

I looked them in the eyes and said, "We'll do it . . . we'll build your TFC."

No Money and No Cell Service

"You told them we'd do what?!"

Susan couldn't believe her ears. I came home from East Africa with a sober understanding of what needed to be done. As I shared what I had seen with the Crisis Aid board, everyone's hearts were moved to action. But the conversation shifted a bit when I told them what I had already committed us to do.

"Yes, I told them we would build a TFC."

"And that has to cost, what, a hundred . . ."

"Yes, a hundred thousand dollars." I figured cutting to the chase would help pull off the conversational Band-Aid for everyone present. Also, I informed them that we had to get moving on this immediately because many of the people we had met were going to die soon if we didn't.

"Pat," said another board member, "we have $350 in our bank account. You know that, right?"

I told them that I knew this to be the case when I promised that we would build the TFC. Even I thought that I sounded crazy and had lost all sense of reason, but what was I supposed to do in a situation of such sheer desperation? All I knew at the time was that doing nothing was *not* an option.

The board wasn't lacking compassion or faith. They were right that we were lacking funds. This was a tense meeting with our team, and some of them were none too happy that I had pledged such a thing to a group of starving people who would die if we didn't come through. Others were against it not because they didn't want to help, but because we had never actually built or operated a TFC before. I had seen it done in other parts of East Africa, but this kind of thing wasn't our specialty. They were afraid that we might kill some of these people in a noble effort to save them.

As you will learn in the pages ahead, dealing with severe malnourishment and starvation is a very specialized field of medicine. We tend to live in such abundance that we have very little clue about the ways a body shuts down—physically and mentally—when it has been deprived of proper nutrition for weeks and months on end. When a group of people has reached a certain stage of starvation, you can't just pull up with a truckload of food and start passing it out on hot plates. You really will kill someone. This has to be done with precision, under the supervision of medical doctors.

So not only were we completely out of our league on attempting to do something like this in the first place, we were also a cool $99,650 short on our budget. Our mailing list consisted of about forty people. The whole thing seemed unbelievably impossible, but we had made a promise (technically, "I" had made the promise, as several people on our team reminded me), and so what was done was done. We knew we couldn't do it alone. We began asking God and people—and then taking whatever tiny steps we could to get started.

I don't want to oversell or undersell this part of the story, especially since it has happened to us so many times over the years, but somehow over the next several weeks, God moved the hearts of people to give like never before towards this endeavor. A hundred thousand dollars showed up in our bank account from various donors who responded to our requests for help. Six weeks later, we were ready to open our first therapeutic feeding center and our work in East Africa was about to officially begin.

More than seventeen years later, we're still there.

There was only one small problem. Our clinic was ready to open in terms of the facility being built and the supplies being on-site, but we had not been able to secure any doctors or nurses to help us get things moving properly. As I said before, helping to bring someone back from the brink of death by starvation is truly a medical process, one not to be taken lightly or without professional help.

We were slated to begin processing incoming patients the next day. It was yet another one of those moments when we had moved as far as we could move. If God didn't do something, we were going to fail miserably—and the consequences for these starving people would be catastrophic.

My prayers in moments like this are probably not what you would think of as "proper" prayers. My life consists of a running dialogue with God, not because I'm special or holy, but precisely because I am not any of those things. I'm just a normal guy who knows that things are not going to happen unless someone stronger than myself intervenes, so I simply ask Him to do so constantly.

"God, what are you going to do about this?" That was the extent of my praying. Honestly, I said it with both frustration and expectation. We had worked so hard to get to this point and the finish line was in sight, yet we lacked what we needed to fully accomplish the mission. In those kinds of moments, I feel a mix of frustration and faith. There is tension there—

and I think it is a tension that many Christians think they shouldn't feel or indulge in. They think that if they have any doubts at all, then they must not have faith.

But faith is not the absence of doubt; faith is continuing forward *through* the doubts. After all, if there is no reason to doubt, then there is also no need for faith. If there are no obstacles in front of us, then why do we need to trust God to help us overcome those obstacles? The presence of doubt must coincide with the presence of faith or else there's nothing to believe and ask for in the first place.

This also means that normal, human emotions will accompany moments of faith. John the Baptist had his doubts, as did Abraham, Jacob, Moses, David, Peter, Paul, and anyone else who has breath in their lungs and a God story. The "saints" didn't always sound or act like saints—they murdered, lied, schemed, cowered, and demanded answers from God. It wasn't their perfect faith that marked their stories. It was God's perfect grace toward them that made it all work, and through their imperfect willingness to keep trusting His plan for their lives, grace perfected their imperfections in ways they never could do on their own.

BUT FAITH IS NOT THE ABSENCE OF DOUBT; FAITH IS CONTINUING FORWARD THROUGH THE DOUBTS.

"Like, seriously, God, what are you going to do about this?"

One of our local friends, Elias, was standing near me when his phone suddenly began ringing in his pocket. At first, I didn't think anything about it because cell phone rings are a common sound to hear, but then it hit me: we were in an area of the country that didn't have any cell coverage, not before that day and not for over ten years since. I think that Elias went through the same sequence of thoughts at the exact same time I did. We looked at each other with puzzled expressions.

"Hello?" Someone was speaking to him on the other end. I obviously couldn't hear what they were saying, but I watched as his face turned white as a sheet. He finally hung up the phone and stood there in a daze.

"Elias, what is going on?" I asked.

"That was our office. A pediatrician and two pediatric nurses showed up today at one of the larger UN NGOs to work at a TFC. They just found out that there was a clerical mistake and they are not needed there, but they have already taken time off from work to be here. They wanted to know if we might need them to work with us for the next three months."

I was speechless, but only for a second. There was no time to hesitate. "Yes, we want them!" When they arrived, we found out that all three of them had extensive experience working at TFCs in Africa. And they didn't cost us a dime—their trip was already fully covered.

Esther

As our TFC got up and running, we faced many ongoing challenges and changes. However, it was one little girl in particular who was not a part of our TFC program that deeply changed the way we viewed and addressed poverty in East Africa.

Her name was Esther.

Esther's mother was not in our program, but we heard about her situation from some of the people working in the medical clinic adjacent to the TFC. We decided to visit the mother to evaluate her needs and see if we could help. What we encountered was another level of unimaginable heartbreak.

When we came into her room, we found out that she had just given birth to triplets. One of them had died at birth. The mother was sitting on a little tiny mat in the middle of the floor—they didn't even have a mattress for her. She was nursing one of her babies, but I couldn't find the third baby. Then I noticed a little bundle over the corner of the room and asked the nurses about it. It was Esther, her third baby, left there to die.

Tragically, since there was so little food, there wasn't enough to feed the mom, so she could not produce milk for both children. Her poor nurses were out of options. This was the level of poverty and lack they were dealing with day in and day out—destitution beyond imagination. They literally had nothing—not even enough to help a mother nurse her own babies.

The whole situation didn't seem real, but it was—and it is common across East Africa. When the mother saw us, she begged us to help. We picked up Esther and told the mother that we would do everything in our power. The mother was still dealing with some medical complications, so she stayed in the clinic while we took the baby back to our facility to attempt to save her life. We were able to leave food at the clinic for the mother as well, to help her recover and to keep her other baby alive.

We were able to save baby Esther and return her to her mother in a few days, along with more food to help her continue to sustain both babies. When she went back to her village, the people couldn't believe their eyes. They knew that one baby had died and that the other was supposed to follow suit, so they expected her to come with only one. When she came home with two healthy babies and extra food, they were overjoyed!

She explained to them what had happened. She didn't tell them about Pat or Dane or Crisis Aid. Rather, she told them about God who sent people with food to save her baby's life—because that's exactly what happened. The people were so overwhelmed by God's kindness that most of them gave their hearts to Christ after hearing the woman's story.

This reminds me of so many stories in Scripture when Jesus showed up in impossible situations, did impossible things, and then sent people home to tell everyone about it.

A Samaritan woman He met at a well didn't even wait for His instruction—she simply ran to her village and shared what He had said to her with everyone there. They all came out to meet Jesus for themselves—and who knows the impact of those interactions.

Another man tormented by evil spirits who lived naked in a graveyard was finally set free from his internal captors when Jesus commanded them to come out of him and enter a herd of pigs. A weird story for sure, but I've seen some weird stories myself—you can't make them up. Sitting clothed and in his right mind, the healed man wanted to go on the road with Jesus. After all, he hadn't exactly been the most popular guy back in town—being publicly naked and violent for a few years while sleeping in tombs will really put a damper on your social life. But Jesus said to him, "'No, go back to your family, and tell them everything God has done for you.' So he went all through the town proclaiming the great things Jesus had done for him" (Luke 8:39).

God did great things for Esther's mom—and she shared those things with those around her. That's the simple way this whole gospel thing is supposed to work, but we tend to overcomplicate it and make it about a lot of other things. It is all too easy to miss opportunities to help someone experience the help and healing of Jesus—and so they never return to tell those in their lives about what happened to them when Jesus sent us to love them. We lack the stories not because they can't happen, but because we are not present where they are happening.

If you want to see miracles, you need to be where miracles are needed.

Every time I see Esther, it reminds me of what Jesus has done and continues to do in all of us. That precious little bundle of sorrow left to die in a dark corner of a forgotten place in this world was seen by a Father who loved her. For the first few years as a little child, she would scream every time she saw me. Today, she is a healthy teenager. She is a reminder that God sees and saves beautiful, invaluable lives just like her.

And just like you.

Asking Better Questions

You can't be successful trying to only affect situations. You've got to affect the people the situations are affecting. People are not only the best motivation to take action; they are also the reward. Getting to know and love people like Esther and her mom is the immeasurable gift that God grants to each of us all around the world. It is not cliché— *they* are one of the ways that God continually reveals His love to me, regardless of what He sends me to do for them. We're all broken people—and it's one God who heals us all, often by bringing our brokenness together in unexpected places.

Our TFC and its processes were far from perfect. We sometimes failed and had to change course, but no matter what you think about Africa or the Middle East or someone hungry in your own backyard, let me tell you that it all begins by really seeing people. That's how God sees you. That's the secret to not only effectiveness, but also fulfillment.

Really seeing people can lead you to do passionate things you never thought you would do. In the next chapter, I will tell you all about a product that helps to save severely malnourished children called Plumpy Nut. For now, just know that when children are starving, this product can mean the difference between life and death.

When we were first getting started in East Africa, I was told that there was a supply of Plumpy Nut in one of the buildings behind the clinic where we were working, but that we couldn't have it. The medical personnel in the clinic were trying to save multiple children dying of starvation, and things weren't going well. They told me that UNICEF was the only organization who could give us permission to get to the life-saving nutrition in that building—and getting that permission would take a long time, especially considering where we were and how much time we had to spare before more children would not be spared. Esther needed the food now, not later. There was no later for her.

Again, these were real children, not pictures. Dane, one of our team members, was with me, and we just couldn't take it.

We walked back to the building, and somehow the lock on the door came off. (I'm not going to tell you how, but you're pretty smart.) In a few minutes, we walked back with a few cases of Plumpy Nut and gave them to the nurses, who were thrilled but befuddled.

Did I steal? I'm really not sure. Probably. Do I regret it? Not at all. I reasoned in my head that my taxes had gone to fund UNICEF, so in some ways, I shared ownership of what was in that tiny building. Regardless, consider this my confession—and know that I'm pretty sure the statute of limitations has expired on this event after all these years.

All I know is that a few children didn't die that day, and while I don't endorse breaking the law, it is high time that the world realizes what has been happening to people in Africa—and takes whatever actions are necessary to affect it. Listen. Give. Pray. Go. Support organizations like Crisis Aid and others who are going places to help people you may never get to meet—people like Esther whose lives literally hang in the balance.

The miraculous opening of our TFC with the doctors calling us on a phone with no service is an incredible story, but the truth of the situation in Africa doesn't usually end with neat little bows and tidy conclusions. God provided what we needed to get started in our first TFC, but we were going to need to remain humble and open to change because nothing about this ongoing situation of poverty and starvation was easy or predictable—it still isn't.

It's all too easy to sum up or dismiss the horrific situations in Africa because they are so vast and so far away. Seeing numbers in the thousands can desensitize us to the conditions of real people. Because we don't have to be affected by what's happening to them, it can feel like it's not real. Out of sight, out of mind. Like a TV show, when we hear new statistics about starving children in Africa or ongoing civil war, we almost respond with, "Oh, yeah, is that still on? I thought they cancelled that."

The problems are ongoing, which means that those willing to pay attention and help must become comfortable with the idea of ongoing work. Crisis Aid is not a Band-Aid—it's a group of people supported by other people who are continually and collectively on a mission together. It's easy to let setbacks discourage you to the extent that you throw up your hands and cry, "What's the point?! We can't help everybody!" We must

CONTINUING FORWARD, EVEN WHEN THE NEEDS SEEM ENDLESS, IS THE KEY TO NOT ONLY MEETING ONE NEED, BUT ALSO BEING A PART OF SYSTEMIC CHANGE FOR MORE PEOPLE AND COMMUNITIES.

refuse to do this. Continuing forward, even when the needs seem endless, is the key to not only meeting one need, but also being a part of systemic change for more people and communities.

Early on, we had about thirty-five severely malnourished children come to our TFC. Even with qualified medical staff in place, the work is delicate and there are no guarantees. Each patient's body is unique, as are their challenges. In addition to these unique issues, most severely malnourished children are loaded down with various bacteria and germs that lie dormant in their bodies. The tragic result of giving their bodies what they most need—proteins, sugars, and the like—is that bacteria also feed on these things, which can cause them to suddenly develop major infections, sometimes leading to sudden cardiac arrest. All because you gave a starving child something to eat.

Over the first several months of our TFC, we lost seven children while trying to save their lives. Yes, all thirty-five would have died if we had done nothing, but seven was far too high of a margin. Seven families lost their precious ones. We knew we needed more knowledge so we could develop better methods to help.

We began looking at the big picture of malnutrition a little more holistically. It was more complex than we had first been able to process or appreciate. We realized that we had served thirty-five children whose mothers brought them in, but there were more like 250 mothers in the village. What was causing this discrepancy?

As we listened to them, we found that most of the mothers had five or six children. Before we came, when one of these children became especially malnourished, the mothers were faced with the impossible conclusion that he or she wasn't going to make it. Just think of how awful that has to be—to have lived for so long in a place where children regularly die of starvation that you have to make this kind of decision to try to save your whole family. Often, the dying child was just left alone in the house to succumb to the inevitable.

This may be hard for Western minds to conceive, but I urge you not to judge. We really have no clue what these families have lived through for generations. Make no mistake, every time one of their children dies, they die a thousand deaths on the inside, just as you or I would if we lost a child. The circumstances are much different, but the loss is very much the same.

Our presence with the TFC had basically dealt with one problem—the one dying child that the mother couldn't support. However, it was not dealing with the rest of the children in these homes who were also malnourished, nor had it dealt with the family as a whole. We began thinking differently about the problem. We began moving from the idea of feeding a child to the concept of finding better ways to support the entire family—children and adults.

Other NGOs shared their data with us. In many TFCs, when a child was rehabilitated and went back home with the parent, they would be sent with an adequate food supply to sustain the medical recovery process for the child only. How do you think that went down? If a mom has more than one starving child, do you think she's going to feed the one and let the others starve to death while they watch? Of course not. So the mothers were dividing the one child's food among the whole family. This would keep the most malnourished child from getting what he or she needed to avoid regression, which often led to the child's death in the long run, even after being treated at the TFC.

It was apparent that our system—the system—wasn't working. We were losing children, and mothers were being put in impossible situations, which often kept them from coming for help. It was time to begin thinking differently. I once heard Tony Robbins talk about a concept that deeply impacted my way of thinking—namely, that we have to learn to ask better questions.

The better question for us was: how do we help a family? This was not a onetime question to ask, but a change to the way we approached relief efforts across the board. We couldn't get caught up in the rut of doing what we had always done. We always try to accomplish whatever mission lies before us, but we also always keep asking ourselves, are there better ways to do this? Is there a bigger problem we're not seeing?

In the beginning, this new question led us to close down our TFC and move instead to a feeding program conducted directly in the homes. We could still treat the most urgently malnourished children at our clinic, if necessary. But more importantly, we sent mothers home with enough food to feed their entire families for a whole month while also requiring visits every two weeks to check on the most severely malnourished children and make sure they were progressing. We tried to take away the impossible decisions that these mothers were having to make—no one should have to choose which of their children live and which ones die.

SEVEN

Asking Better Questions

East Africa

The journey that led us to ask better questions in East Africa arose because of the sheer number of children who were starving. I have been all over the world and have seen poverty on many levels, but I had only seen one child—Zorha in Afghanistan, who weighed eleven pounds at eighteen months—who was as bad as the children we were finding by the thousands in East Africa.

As I said before, the term "severe malnutrition" means that without intervention, a child will soon die. There is more at stake than just survival, though we obviously begin with attempting to save lives. Depending upon the amount of time spent in a state of severe malnutrition, even if a child recovers, more than 90 percent of the time, he or she is going to suffer cognitive and developmental issues that persist for life. This is a result of the brain being deprived of essential nutrients during key moments of development.

A child who faces the uphill climb of being stunted in one of these important areas of development becomes even more marginalized in a culture where the challenges are already quite daunting. He or she will struggle to mentally and emotionally engage in adult tasks and roles—and to be clear, this is all simply because they don't have enough food to eat. Food scarcity is the first domino that knocks down the others.

I spend much of my life trying to help people realize that above all else this is a food problem—and it's been going on for multiple generations in East Africa. Because of a lack of food, the vast snowball of poverty, malnourishment, and hopelessness has become so huge that thousands of East Africans get crushed before they've ever had a chance to start truly living. This is not just about preventing death, but also saving lives—lives of real people who not only breathe, but can also think, work, grow, marry, play, and have the potential to become everything that we all want our children to become.

This is why tools for evaluating malnourishment are so very important. They help us identify those at the highest risk as early as possible, thus hopefully giving the child a chance to be treated before permanent damage sets in and affects his or her life moving forward.

One key tool is called an MUAC band. MUAC stands for Middle Upper Arm Circumference. It is a color-coded plastic band that is wrapped around a child's arm halfway between the top of their shoulder and their elbow. If it reads red, they are severely malnourished. Yellow means they are moderately malnourished. Green means they are relatively healthy from a food scarcity perspective. These tools are used by UNICEF as well as the World Health Organization.

Anytime someone comes to work with us in East Africa, I have them partake in food distribution because I want them to experience both the work and the people. We will pair them off to spend time measuring the children with the MUAC bands. This is a beautiful sight to behold because it gives them face-to-face interaction with the children and their mothers.

People seem to grow weary of seeing starving babies on television, but holding one in your arms is a completely different and life-changing experience. It is a life-changing experience for many who have visited one of our sites. I have heard that some of our teams tried to pull the MUAC band extra tight so that the children they were helping would be given more food.

Truth is, we already knew what the children would be getting before anyone used the MUAC bands on them, but the volunteers' desire to maximize what they receive demonstrates the power of showing the love and care of God to real people in real life, which mirrors another of our core values. They already loved these children so much that they were eager to give them as much as possible.

Believing God for Too Little

There is so much good that so many people do to affect the issue of hunger in East Africa, but one of the reasons I'm writing this book is that I'm sick of the problem. I'm tired of trying to solve this hunger pandemic using the same methods. I've seen thousands upon thousands of starving children over almost two decades in the area, and there seems to be no end in sight.

Again, we must ask better questions. We have been wrestling with questions like: why is it so hard just to keep these children alive? Shouldn't survival be the easiest part? Shouldn't we have made more progress in affecting the root of the problem? Should we continually keep trying to maximize the effectiveness of the same ways we've been responding to this problem for years? The truth is, we were struggling just to keep children alive because there were so many who were malnourished.

Fast forward to the present, we feel like we've formulated a better plan—and it all began with the tragic death of a four-year-old girl. Her picture is the only way to do justice to the severity of her condition (see photo section). I was at one of our food distribution centers when I turned around and a father thrust a little girl into my arms. When I looked at her, I was speechless. She felt as light as a feather, as if she was wasting away into nothingness before my very eyes.

I looked at her father—his expression reflected the sheerest desperation I have ever seen. I could tell that he had been wearing his clothes for several years. We were in a very poor region, but this guy was the poorest of the poor. We had found the epicenter of the poverty where it was most severe—and the precious human evidence lay barely breathing in my arms.

I asked around and found out that this family was not in our feeding program. The truth is—and this has nothing to do with race—because we look different from what many locals are used to seeing, they will often come because they assume we are here to help. This is not some white man's rescue syndrome. We are cultural anomalies to them, but if it means that families will bring dying children to us when they won't take them anywhere else, we're perfectly content to stick out like sore thumbs all day long.

This man had come simply because he had heard we were there. I could tell that we were probably out of time, so I had the translator ask the father if he could come with us immediately to the hospital with the child. He said yes. I sent them with a pastor and another team member to the hospital, along with the money they would need for medical care. We stayed on and continued the food distribution.

When our team members came back that night, they told us more of the father's story. He had lost his wife a year earlier to a simple infection that any common antibiotic would have treated. Three months before showing up at our site, he had lost two children to starvation—and he was losing this one. All told, he would be left with only one child. He was spending his time scavenging for work as day laborer—and if he was lucky, he was able to come home with fifty cents as a days' wages.

Many days, he wasn't so lucky.

Three days later, we received the call that we expected: the child had died. We weren't surprised, but it was still a gut-wrenching moment. I can remember standing there with the father at the distribution site. I turned to our country director and said, "What the hell is going on? We've got to start asking a different question! What we're asking now is obviously not solving this problem!"

This moment of utter torment caused us to get our minds rolling in different directions. We didn't necessarily discover something new, but we began to emphasize something we already knew: not only do these people have no food, but they also have no opportunities. This is such a hard concept for the American mind because so often, and errantly so, we instinctively believe that anyone can start from nothing, work hard, fight hard, and eventually make themselves into something. This industrious idea of work ethic only works because we believe that America is "the land of opportunity." And in many ways, especially compared to the poverty in East Africa, it is.

Our mindset about opportunity is completely foreign (no pun intended) to the people living in poverty in East Africa. There is often literally nothing for them to do. There are no businesses. No one's yard to mow for a few extra bucks. No minimum wage jobs. No way for them to engage in proper agriculture because they don't have the money to buy seeds or equipment, even if the soil doesn't dry up with one of the many droughts.

There is an old expression we all know well: *give a man a fish, you feed him for a day. Teach a man to fish, you feed him for a lifetime.* From a metaphorical standpoint, there are people in East Africa who do not understand fishing at all—that is, being able to do something to improve your own station. There is a disconnect there that has existed for generations because no one has been able to do anything to provide for themselves. Can you imagine this mindset—the idea that no matter what you dream of, work hard at, or set your sights on, you will never be able to earn enough of a living to keep your children from starving?

We began thinking about *this* problem—the lack of hope for any opportunity. We needed to help resurrect hope for so many highly intelligent, industrious people who had never even been able to dream about a minimum wage job. Their brains had stopped hoping for things like that, so when problems arose, they already knew that they could do nothing about them, just like their parents and their parents' parents.

INSTEAD OF JUST STRUGGLING TO KEEP THEM ALIVE, WE BEGAN TO PRAY AND DREAM ABOUT HELPING THEM TRULY LIVE.

Instead of just struggling to keep them alive, we began to pray and dream about helping them truly live. We felt God leading us to begin offering them glimpses of hope they had never entertained before—to demonstrate to them what was possible so they might have hope to reach for something. It wasn't their fault that they had never had this chance—they needed someone to love them in all areas, which meant that we had to get busy changing the ways we do our work.

One idea we have yet to fully get off the ground involves coffee growers. Some of the people in the area who do have a minimum income source grow coffee, so we have begun thinking of ways to teach them to multiply their yields—conceivably by ten times or more—while also producing a superior coffee.

Coffee farmers remain in poverty because they only have one coffee harvest a year, which means that they have no income the rest of the time. We had an agricultural specialist from Australia come up with the idea of planting other cash crops in the spaces between their coffee trees, crops they could harvest three or four times a year. Besides more profit, these other crops would help to circulate nutrients back into the soil for the coffee trees. With the extra crops, they could either eat what they grow or sell their extra yield to buy food. Again, we are trying to help them begin thinking differently about what they have and what they can do with it.

Earlier, I referenced a product called Plumpy Nut. It is a peanut-based paste high in fat, carbohydrates, and protein.

There are several similar products out there, and they are game changers for children suffering from acute malnutrition. These are called RUTFs, or ready-to-use therapeutic foods. They can be given to any child over six months of age. I have seen children on their deathbeds who started eating RUTFs and were up running and playing within thirty days' time. These are miracle foods, which is why *60 Minutes* and other news organizations have done reports about their benefits.

Our problem is that RUTFs are in high demand in the area, so distribution is usually controlled by the UN in African countries. This can make them hard to come by, especially when you need them right now. They are also very expensive—costing between four dollars and five dollars a day to feed a child. That may not sound like much at first, but multiply that number by four thousand children a day and it quickly adds up. We've used them before, but not regularly because of the price.

We began to ask better questions. What else do we have access to that has similar nutritional value? We had one facility where multiple children were very bad off, so every day for about six weeks, we made sure they had an egg and an eight-ounce glass of raw milk in their diet. The before and after pictures of these children were shocking. They looked like different people! We began to treat their mothers with the same diet, and when I received their pictures, I couldn't believe my eyes.

All from an egg and a glass of milk. This generated an idea that we think is a game changer for these poverty-stricken families in East Africa: dairy farms. Not only would they be able to produce milk for our feeding programs, but since there is also a shortage of milk in the area, the dairy farms would create a supply for the milk demand, growing into a business model that provides a service to the surrounding community, as well as jobs for those who need them the most.

Like most things I dream up, I had no idea what I was doing. Where would we start such a thing? The truth is, God had been putting the location in my literal path for quite some time, I just hadn't realized it. For years, we had traveled up and down a certain back road during our food distributions, passing a piece of hilly property dotted with gorgeous trees that had a beautiful river snaking through it. Each time, we would stop to take in the beauty, dreaming of owning it one day.

When the idea of the first dairy farm began to develop, I went home and told a few people about that piece of land. Word spread, and the next thing we knew, a donor had given enough money to buy the property. Then another donor gave enough money to build the barn and its infra-structure. Today, we have about fifty cows and more than fifteen calves that have been born on that property, thus growing by the day our operation to serve those in need.

But it doesn't stop there. Why? Because better questions beget better answers. When we began asking better questions about dealing with systemic issues of poverty and more affordable food sources to treat malnutrition, our pitch for the dairy farm introduced another question: how will we distribute what we are producing from the dairy farms in an effective, medically sound methodology? We dreamed of and began pitching the idea of a medical clinic on the same piece of property. This would be a more permanent solution as opposed to the makeshift clinics we sometimes erected at temporary food distribution sites.

At the time, we were dreaming of building a small, five-room lean-to. This would be a place where we could keep and treat children for twenty-four to forty-eight hours, but it wouldn't have any long-term functionality. Because medical care was so non-existent in the area, it would be better than nothing. However, I began telling our team and the doctors working with us that I feared we might be believing God for too little.

A short time later, a donor visited our feeding program. He asked us what we wanted to do, so we told him

I BEGAN TELLING OUR TEAM AND THE DOCTORS WORKING WITH US THAT I FEARED WE MIGHT BE BELIEVING GOD FOR TOO LITTLE.

about the dairy farm and our idea for a permanent clinic. He asked us to take him to the property. After a few minutes of seeing the beautiful area, he asked us to send him a proposal for the clinic, so we did—and this time, we were careful *not* to ask for too little.

HOW CAN WE ASK GOD TO DO THE IMPOSSIBLE IF IT'S NOT REALLY IMPOSSIBLE?

We gave him a proposal for a two-story clinic that would ultimately house twenty beds. He took it back to his supporters in the States and they said yes. Today, the medical clinic is up and running. We have two pediatricians on staff and many nurses, some of whom also serve as cooks and come from one of our other special programs.

In the next chapter, you'll realize why they are so special.

God is continuing to challenge us not to shortchange our belief or our requests to Him for his intervention. After the clinic was up and running, I was walking with one of the doctors again and it hit me—we shouldn't be done.

"Look at this clinic that we just built," I told him. "Look at this dairy farm and these people who are receiving food and hope for their future."

"I know," he replied, "It's amazing."

"Yes, it is, but I think we should repent."

He looked confused. "Repent for what?"

"I think we're still guilty of believing God for too little. What if we asked God for what we really want here? What would it be?"

He thought for a moment. "It would be a full-scale, pediatric hospital with over a hundred beds. Fully staffed and ready to address any issue that comes our way."

I smiled. That was a dream far beyond our ability or means. It felt like insanity, which felt right in some weird way. We prayed about it right there in that field.

At the time of this writing, we have just finished the first building of the hospital and we secured the funding for the second building. I still sometimes experience worry over where the money will come from. However, I generally find myself asking God for bigger things. He always comes through. Real faith can't exist without real challenges and real doubts. How can we ask God to do the impossible if it's not really impossible?

Medical Miracles

One of the most glaring places that the impossible intersects our efforts is in the medical needs of the people we meet. Many of our trips focus on these medical needs, and we've seen God do the impossible in so many people's lives. I will never forget a five-year-old girl named Lemlem whose mother brought her to us because she had no other options. She had broken her ankle when she was two years old, and because of their abject poverty, the family was never able to have the break properly repaired. Walking was almost impossible for her, so going to school was a dream that she and her mother never thought would come true.

One day during one of our medical missions trips, Lemlem's mother heard we were working in her area and came to see us. She had not been prescreened to come to the clinic we had set up. We treated almost four thousand people in five days, and Lemlem was not going to be one of them. I was standing there talking to our country director when I saw this mother, carrying Lemlem in her arms, approach one of our team members seeking help. The team member pointed to me.

The mother walked in my direction and put Lemlem down. She then crawled to us, stopping about three feet from me. She looked into my eyes and gave me the biggest smile I had ever seen. That was all it took to melt my heart. After talking to the mother, we went to visit their small home. They had very little—a few cooking pots, a couple of benches, and a mat to sleep on. I asked where they stored their food. The mother took me into a room that acted as a kitchen where she would build a small fire on the dirt. She took the lid off a small cooking pot, revealing a few rotten potatoes in the bottom. This was all the food she had for herself and her five children. Her husband had left her several years earlier.

God's timing is always perfect. A few weeks after the

medical team returned to the United States, our in-country team took Lemlem to a hospital where an American ortho- pedic surgeon was treating patients. He had spent many years serving the poor in this region. After examining her, he thought he could correct the problem, but time was of the essence. If the mother had waited another few months, Lemlem's bones would have grown to the point of becoming completely unrepairable.

After several surgeries and several sets of braces, Lemlem was able to start school for the first time in her life. It was a true miracle. She moved from having no future due to the limitations of her disability to having one that is bright. Lemlem is now seventeen years old, and she runs and walks without any limp. She is completely healed! She is also doing excellent in school.

All we had to do was show up and say yes to picking up one of the cutest little girls we had ever seen. God did the rest.

Two years later, we hosted another American medical team for five days in a remote area of East Africa. On the fourth day of the clinic, another miracle was set into motion. This would be one of the greatest physical healings I have ever seen.

A girl named Hiwot was brought to us with the most severe series of tumors

ALL WE HAD TO DO WAS SHOW UP AND SAY YES. GOD DID THE REST.

imaginable. They literally covered her upper torso and neck. The photo we have included in the photo section is the only way to do her condition justice. She was suffering in so many ways. When we came into her area to offer medical care, she had not been included because we had not seen her in the prescreening process. Yet her father heard that we were there and brought her out of absolute desperation. When our doctors examined her, they said that if she were left in her current state, the tumors would cut off her air supply before the cancer could take her life. Her condition was literally choking her to death.

We decided to take her to the capital city, where a Korean hospital agreed to examine her. It was an eight-hour drive. We left her at the hospital and secured her father a hotel room for the week, along with money for food. The hospital doctors said they thought they could help, but there were no guarantees. We told them to do what they could.

Hiwot underwent a series of surgeries, chemotherapy, and radiation treatments. The photos of her today are the only accurate evidence of her transformation; no words will suffice. Hiwot had no future other than an agonizing death at the young age of sixteen. Today, she has graduated from college with a degree in computer science, is married, and has a beautiful baby. She now works full-time for Crisis Aid in one of our pediatric clinics.

We knew that including the photo of her tumors would

reveal a very personal and painful matter that could embarrass her, something we would never want to do. When I asked her if we could include it, she said that if it could bring glory to God, she was all in. God is doing impossible things—and there are so many more things to ask Him for. Asking Him for the impossible is not an act of blind faith. As we learn to ask better, more honest questions, we invite God deeper into our specific needs and our own ways of thinking. We invite Him to help us address not just sickness or poverty, but also the inherited mindset adopted by so many generations of families stuck in poverty with no hope of escape. Now, many are beginning to hope in what God can do in them— and what they might be able to pursue in their own lives and for others as God keeps sending people who love them and are willing to stand with them in repairing the breaches all around them.

After all, that's what God promises to us in Isaiah 58— that "your ancient ruins shall be rebuilt; you shall raise up the foundations of many generations; you shall be called the *repairer of the breach*, the restorer of streets to dwell in" (ESV, verse 12, emphasis mine). This breach is not just physical—it is foundational, and it exists all over the world, not just in places considered to be "Third World." There are just as many mental, spiritual, and physical breaches in the United States, even with the wealth that abounds here.

In East Africa, God is meeting needs on all levels, including the renewing of minds to be open to hope and possibility. We are now asking from Him something that seems far beyond anything conceivably possible in our lifetimes: to lead us to permanently break the cycle of poverty that has existed in this region of Africa for many generations.

And don't forget that this all started with the tragic death of a four-year-old girl.

We have already seen the impossible occur many times—why not this? Why not now? And why not through us? And since you're sitting here in these pages with me, why not with you working alongside us in some way? If your ability to help seems impossibly small or insignificant, let me tell you about one of the nurses at the clinic—a special one whom we will call by the name Safiyya. If she can work toward this cause, then I promise you can too.

You see, not too long ago, Safiyya was a sex slave trapped in a red-light district with thousands of other teenage girls.

Welcome to Hell

"I think we're going to hang out with prostitutes tonight."

It was probably one of the strangest sentences I had ever spoken to my wife, but by 2006, very little surprised her anymore. At that point in time, most of our work in East Africa centered upon the feeding programs, but as I was speaking with a guy who runs a ministry serving children living on the streets, I sensed God nudging me in a very unexpected direction.

"Ask him about prostitution."

It seemed odd, so I hesitated. Then I heard it again.

"Ask him about prostitution."

"Uh, would you mind telling me about prostitution in this area?" No doubt, the question seemed like an abrupt left turn in our conversation, but it was another sharp turn that God was initiating. My friend could sense it as well.

"Many prostitutes live down in the red-light district." He went on to describe the deplorable conditions in which they were living and the unspeakable poverty and abuse they were suffering as sex slaves. Most of them were young teenage girls—slaves caught in a system that offered them no conceivable avenue of escape. Mind you, the term "sex trafficking" was just beginning to become part of our Western vernacular. At that time, there were very few highly organized efforts to rescue girls trapped in such indescribable exploitation.

Back in the mid-1990s, I had read disturbing reports of child prostitution in Thailand, and I took a trip there to investigate. I spent a day with ministry leaders who told me stories and showed me photographs that still haunt me to this day. I came home and tried to help with fundraising for the cause, but for whatever reason, we weren't able to get much traction. It seemed that it wasn't quite time for us to become fully involved.

But the seed had been planted.

Ten years later in East Africa, that seed was sprouting. As my friend told Dane and me more about the red-light district, I asked, "Can you take us there tonight?" He paused for a moment, obviously thinking through the logistical and safety challenges of taking people who look like *us* into a place like *that*.

"Sure, I'll take you . . . if you really want to go." I was glad that Dane was with me, because we had no idea what we would see or experience.

Western perception of places like East Africa often only entails rural villages with dirt roads, no running water, and a small population surrounded by dense vegetation. As you have read from our stories up to now, many parts of Africa do indeed look like this, but the major cities are quite different—and the poverty within them is unique to urban Africa. The city we were visiting at the time was home to nearly four million inhabitants, roughly the same population as the city of Los Angeles.

I will never forget my first exposure to urban Africa. Many parts of the city did indeed have dirt roads, but most of the roads were paved with cut stones. Most people walked, but cars and motorcycles also bustled throughout the endless streets, intersections, and roundabouts. These were all situated below large highway bridges and an ever-expanding yet fragile infrastructure. I was riding through a city larger than most Americans will ever live in, with countless street corners dotted with Internet cafes, small businesses, and advertisements for everything under the sun. Dogs and goats lazily, but seemingly intentionally, meandered down the sidewalks as if on their way to jobs with bosses who couldn't care less when they clocked in. Street kids were everywhere.

Wide sidewalks littered with crumbling stones from adjacent buildings hosted a very diverse population of people—some coming, some going, and some just standing there leaned up against various walls and railings, smoking cigarettes or talking on cell phones. Small makeshift shops and makeshift homes were built into the lower levels of the buildings lining the streets, claimed and crafted by endless sheets of thin, corrugated tin puzzled together with tattered, misshapen pieces of canvas and tarp. The people were just trying to survive as they lived, worked, and moved amid a kaleidoscope of dusty, faded colors—each just trying to find his or her way in the world.

The problem was, as I was about to find out, some of the people in this city weren't allowed to search for their own way in this world. A certain cruel and shameful *way* was being forced upon them. Many young girls lived in the red-light district, one of the largest of its kind in the world, nestled within seemingly endless alleyways. Even the churches in this city shunned them—worse even still was the fact that the girls knew this. Their culture and society were either exploiting, ignoring, or rejecting them. We were determined to treat them differently.

We were perhaps the first Westerners to ever go there—and as usual, we didn't really blend in. As we unloaded out of the van and began walking, a rancid smell immediately overtook us, evidence of the raw sewage running in the alleyways. We didn't have much time to process the smell because before we knew it, we had reached the outskirts of the place where thousands of girls were living—thousands of beautiful little daughters and sisters being sexually abused and exploited as they slept just feet away from streams of raw sewage.

I usually put myself in the shoes of those I serve, but this time, I thought of my own daughter in their shoes, which was indescribably worse.

Each girl lived in her own tiny tin shack leaning up against the next shack in the row, a sequence stretching for what seemed like miles. Each shack was only about six feet wide and eight feet deep, just large enough to house a bed and sometimes a small table. Many of them didn't have electricity, and none of them had running water.

Silhouetted by whatever light could shine in this dark place were young girls in short dresses standing in the doorways of their "homes." From their thresholds, they gazed with curiosity and fear at our small entourage. This was a whole other world of suffering that all of us had been privileged to never even see, much less experience. But I knew that Jesus had walked these alleyways countless times—and it was becoming even more abundantly clear that He knew exactly where (and to whom) He was sending us that night.

As we walked, we came upon a group of five girls. We began talking to them, and since we were making a scene, we asked if we could go into one of their rooms. As we were going inside, I suddenly felt drawn like a laser beam to another girl walking past us by herself. There were people standing everywhere, but it felt like she was the only one I could focus on. I asked the interpreter to ask the girl if she would be willing to come inside with the others to meet with us. She agreed.

There we were—in the middle of a sex slave's quarters with five girls, an interpreter, and another teenage girl whom we shall call Zuri. We began telling all of them about God's love for them, but I just couldn't get away from the fact that I knew God had something special for Zuri right then. I looked her in the eyes and, through the interpreter, began telling her about God's love for her specifically. I told her that there were things God had planned for her that she hadn't even yet begun to dream about. I also told her that His heart was broken for her because He saw what she was going through every night.

Zuri and the others listened intently to my less-than-articulate talk. It didn't matter how I said it—Jesus was speaking it directly into their innermost places of broken-ness and shame, just as He has done for me so many times. I finally asked them if they wanted to accept Jesus' invitation to come into their hearts right then. All of them said yes. We prayed together, and right there in the midst of unspeakable atrocities, God did an unspeakable work of grace in their lives—and in mine. But He wasn't finished yet—not by a long shot.

After we prayed, I immediately felt God lead me to baptize Zuri. It seemed like such an impractical thing to do for so many reasons. Could someone get a pot filled with water? Wouldn't this draw more attention to us? Beyond that, I had never baptized anyone before.

But I had come too far to stop listening to God now. I asked her if she was willing to be baptized, and she said yes. Before I knew it, someone showed up with a pot of water. We stepped back out into the alleyway, and Zuri leaned down so I could pour the water over her head. I probably did not say all the things you're supposed to say at a baptism. It didn't matter—Jesus was in charge, and He was doing a much better job than I could have ever done.

When Zuri straightened back up with the water dripping from her head, it was as if she was a different person. She beamed with the brightest smile I'd ever seen in my life. She seemed to literally light up the alley with a glow that everyone could tell "wasn't from around here." I was blown away by the undeniable change in her countenance, but I was even more surprised by what came out of my mouth next.

"Would you like to leave here tonight?"

It was an impossible, yet "better" question I never knew

I would ask—and I couldn't have dreamed what God was going to do in the lives of Zuri and thousands of others who would follow.

EIGHT

The Power of Yes

East Africa and Cambodia

"Yes."

I couldn't believe it. What were we going to do with her? "Is it safe?" I asked.

"Yes, my owner is not around." Her words broke my heart. No child should have to worry about an owner. This emboldened me to see this through. Now more than ever, doing nothing was most certainly not an option.

"Go get your stuff and come back here. We'll wait for you." Zuri returned in about ten minutes with everything she owned in a plastic bag like a Walmart sack. She followed us to the van, where we loaded up and left. I can't imagine what she must have been thinking as she watched the red-light district become smaller and smaller behind us.

As the interpreter spoke with her, we learned that she was only sixteen years old. Her family had all died or abandoned her, so she had been living in the red-light district for the past five years. I shuddered to think that she started there as an eleven-year-old. We literally had nowhere to take her, so we prepared a place for her to sleep in an office for the few first nights.

> NEVER UNDERESTIMATE THE POWER OF ONE YES. ULTIMATELY, ALL GOD REALLY NEEDS FROM US IS OUR YES.

This was the beginning of a new dream and a new work—the work of rescuing girls who were sex slaves and helping them take steps toward new lives. Zuri's courageous walk out of the red-light district set us on the journey of building a home where she and others who were being victimized in the red-light districts could live after we rescued them.

And it all began with a yes. If Zuri had said no to us that night, I truly believe that we would have dropped the whole endeavor to rescue girls enslaved in sex trafficking. Her "yes" unleashed something in heaven, and God began moving on her behalf in a different way. Her "yes" put her and many other people on a path toward freedom and a life of purpose. It also put us on that path with her.

God knew who to send walking past us that night. She didn't know the other five girls, and they didn't know her. Yet she said yes to the invitation of two white guys who invited her into another prostitute's room. Who knows what she was thinking? I have no idea, but God knew—and the power of that one "yes" began an unimaginable path forward.

It reminded me of the second time I said "I do"—another big yes. I was so scared of what might happen, but I had no idea what God would do in our lives "from this day forward." Besides being married again to the love of my life, God also restored our family and sent us down a path of helping others. Without that yes, there would be no Crisis Aid. There would be no stories of helping others. There would no story of inviting Zuri into the safety of knowing Christ and experiencing freedom.

Never underestimate the power of one yes. Ultimately, all God really needs from us is our yes.

Zuri was rescued in December of 2006. We went back into the red-light district in January of 2007. There were three of us this time, and as usual, we were attracting a lot of attention. As we walked up, once again, it was as if my eyes were drawn to one girl standing in the middle of dozens of others. I doubted that this could be happening again; I thought I was just being crazy and making stuff up in my head. I tried to ignore it and walked about fifteen or twenty yards past her when I just couldn't shake the feeling any longer.

We walked back and began speaking with her—and this time, we can use her real name: Melasech. Since a crowd was developing around us again, we asked if we could speak with her inside her room. It was a typical shack in the district—

a bed and a small table. On the wall at the foot of her bed was a framed painting of Jesus praying in the Garden of Gethsemane. I struck up a conversation about the painting.

"Do you believe in God?"

"Yes," she replied.

"That's great—He believes in you too. Do you ever pray to Him?" Her eyes filled with tears.

"Every time I have a man in here, I pray to God to rescue me." She went on to explain that every time she was being raped, she looked at this picture the entire time. I tried to imagine myself being in her place, and it was impossible for me to grasp the utter hell she had experienced every day for years on end.

My heart was broken for her. "God loves you so much, and He sees what you're going through. He sent us here to your country to help. We're creating a program for girls like you to be able to get out of here."

She had stopped crying and had become more stoic, which confused me at the time. "God will never rescue me," she finally mumbled. I'm just a prostitute." She said it again several times. In fact, it was her response to anything I said.

I finally asked, "Would you like to leave here tonight?"

"No, I can't." Melasech seemed resolute, and we didn't want to overwhelm or push her too hard, so we gave her the translator's phone number and told her how much God loved her and how much we wanted to help her. After giving her some money so she would not have to work for several days, we left.

I was scheduled to fly back to the United States a couple days later. Our whole team was working hard to figure out what we were going to do with Zuri—and how we were going to establish a home for others. We were trying to get her checked out and treated from a medical perspective, as well as evaluate what kind of education she might have had. She was in the sixth grade when she was forced into prostitution.

Amid all this, the translator's phone rang. It was Melasech. She said that she wanted to talk to me again—right now. This time, we offered to send someone to pick her up and bring her to us. She agreed.

Our second conversation was much the same as the first one. I kept telling her about God's love for her and His plan for better things in her life. This time, she responded only by repeatedly asking a single question: "Is it really true?"

I kept telling her yes and reiterating what I had been saying, but she kept asking the same question. Again, I needed to ask a better, more direct question of her, so I did. "What do you mean by that?"

"Could God really forgive me? Because I'm nothing but a prostitute." She had been hearing us, but it was too much for her to believe over the shame she felt not just for what she had done, but for who she thought she had become.

"You're not a prostitute," I said. "That's not who you are—that's just what you've been forced to do. But hear me: it is not who you are."

This time, Melasech said nothing. I didn't know if that was a good or a bad thing, so I kept going. "Would you like for us to rescue you out of the red-light district?"

"I'm not sure," she replied.

The better question hit me again. "Okay, why don't we start here instead: would you like to give your life to Jesus?"

Finally, she answered with a yes. We prayed a simple prayer, and right then and there, Melasech accepted for the first time the One who truly saw her and truly loved her, no matter what she thought about herself. The moment was holy—and she was immediately transformed. She smiled, maybe for the first time in years.

"I'm ready to leave now."

Just like that, everything had shifted. I had to go to the airport, so the team accompanied her back to get her things. I had come to East Africa to keep feeding people, but I left compelled to rescue all the girls who were sex slaves in that country and around the world. Melasech was sixteen years old and had been enslaved for four years. Hell began when she was only twelve years old. Something had to change.

The Glorious Unknown

Most of us are a little tentative about the unknown, but for these girls living in the red-light district, the unknown held so much for them—they just didn't know it. Our job was not only to provide a place and a path to safety and life for them, but to first and foremost open their minds up to the possibility that lay outside of the red-light districts and the only lives they had ever known. It was a similar hope deficiency that we were facing on the food scarcity front, though for very different reasons. A lack of hope truly is a universal problem—and in the case of these young girls, hopelessness was literally enslaving them to a life of unspeakable pain and abuse.

To this day, our work with sex trafficking continues because the problem is much bigger than most people in the world realize. By February of 2007, we had rescued three more girls. A few months later, we had rescued a few more of their friends. It was a word-of-mouth process. Hope began to spread among the only people these girls could trust up to that point in time: one another.

When we had seven girls living in various places, it became clear that developing any kind of program to help them was going to take more time. So instead of waiting, we rented out our first home and moved all seven girls into it. Over the years, the homes where the girls lived came to be known as the Refuge Homes. Our goal continues to be to rescue 15,000 girls from the red-light district. Over the past ten years, we've rescued hundreds. At the time of this writing, we just completed a new home that can house one hundred girls, thirty staff, and forty children. It is huge, but again, it is only a tiny speck compared to the vast problem. Even so, we rejoice in these steps and keep asking God for much, much bigger things. We began to examine not just what we were getting the girls *out of*, but also what we were getting them *out to*. This is not a grammatical error, though my staff was a bit confused the first time I said it. This was just another better question scenario. Instead of focusing only on what we were rescuing them from, we needed to equally focus on where they would go once they had been rescued. Instead of only trying to eliminate the negatives of their past, we needed to aim toward the positives of their future.

There were times when girls wanted to get out, but we didn't have room for them or the finances to rescue. There is no worse feeling than driving away and knowing that you couldn't take everyone who wanted to go. Several years into our work, we had opened eight homes and were housing more than eighty girls. Rent and other costs continued to skyrocket, which led us to realize that we needed to ask better questions and pivot to an additional model to help more girls right now, even if we couldn't get them into homes all at once.

This led us to establish a daytime program called Mercy Chapel that allows any girl from the red-light district to learn a trade. In addition to biblical instruction, the girls also learn sewing, hairdressing, computer skills, cooking, weaving, leather crafts, and more. It is a ten-month program that ends with an apprenticeship experience with a local employer during the final thirty days of the program. The result is that most of these girls graduate from Mercy Chapel having already secured a job through their apprenticeships. The sad reality is that, during the program, they still work in the red-light district at night, but they have hope that in a manner of months, they will get out for good. When they graduate, they are able to leave and pursue a different kind of life.

Many people wonder if we encounter much resistance from those who are enslaving these girls. We did at first, but at this point, they know what we are doing and the sad reality is that there are so many girls being funneled into this horrible system that they are not that worried about our efforts. They have plenty of others behind these to exploit.

For the most part, the girls are not physically confined to the red-light district. They could walk out tomorrow, but they think of themselves as indentured bondservants who owe a debt to their pimps—a debt they can never pay off. They think they have to do this because someone they owe expects them to. This is why they expect to stay in this state of being for life. Of course, they are also terrified of what the pimp would do to them if they leave on their own and are caught. I talked to one girl standing in her doorway who told me that the thought of leaving had never crossed her mind. When you consider how embedded these systems are in their psyches, you begin to understand how these precious girls begin to believe that this is the life they must live.

We walk into their lives and tell them that God has a better plan for them—and we ask them if they want to hear about it.

One of these conversations began with a yes and led to another incredible story of redemption. The young nurse I mentioned in the last chapter, Safiyya, was one of the first fifteen girls we rescued from the red-light district. She had faced so much hardship in her life that during her first three weeks with us, she tried to commit suicide multiple times. Hope was hard for her to receive and accept.

But God had plans for Safiyya, which included graduating from high school and going to college to study nursing. At her college graduation, she had two tickets to give away to guests. One went to her mother. The other went to me. Imagine my joy and honor to sit with four thousand East Africans in an auditorium, celebrating the achievement of Safiyya and the other graduates. Also imagine the way I stood out in that crowd.

Safiyya now works for us at the clinic—a complete reversal of her life. She helps to bring healing to others. She recently married, though we were not able to attend because of COVID. Regardless, Safiyya is yet another story of God's willingness to use one simple yes to change life after life. One yes can lead to hope for many.

Another precious girl named Asha was sold by her parents to a local witch doctor at the tender age of eight. She lived in a literal hell for six years before finally finding a chance to run away. But her brave attempt to escape did not lead her to freedom. Instead, she found herself trapped in sexual slavery. But God saw Asha, and He sent us to ask her if she wanted a new life.

She said yes.

In 2009, we were able to rescue her from the red-light district and into a Refuge Home. She was illiterate and had no concept of dreaming for her future. She was obviously withdrawn and afraid. But over time and through the love being shown to her, Jesus began healing her wounds. Soon, she accepted Him into her life and said, "I was lost, but now God has changed my life, and I will serve Him forever." We had no idea the fullness of that statement or what was to come. Asha began taking courses through Mercy Chapel , eventually accomplishing her goal of becoming the top graduate of Mercy Chapel's first graduating class. After being promoted to teacher's assistant in the hair dressing department, she began pursuing a new vocation.

She began taking night classes, beginning at kindergarten and progressing all the way through high school. She excelled academically to the point that she was also the top graduate from that school. All this occurred when she had been illiterate only a few years before.

Today, Asha works for Crisis Aid as an advocate and an active participant in rescuing other girls from sexual slavery.

She served as the Assistant Coordinator of Mercy Chapel and then the Coordinator in the same Refuge Home where she first lived after being rescued. She personally goes back into the red-light district to bring other girls out, inviting them into our Refuge Homes and the Mercy Chapel program. Asha said yes to hope—and now many others are saying yes to hope through the work God continues to do in her life.

Asha recently said, "I've been at this Refuge Home for five years and am now working as a normal citizen. These have been the best five years of my life. I am very happy and trying to give back by helping other girls. When I summarize my life here, I've found my true identity, and by finding myself, something heavenly. Above all, I have learned much love."

Asha shares her testimony with the girls who are still struggling, helping them understand the possibilities that await them. After all, she knows better than anyone what it truly means to be set free. She understands the power of hope.

Hope is contagious in any language, and that's not just some cliché phrase for your next Facebook meme—it's true. After we began to establish homes and programs for girls, word began spreading about the amazing success we were having, and we began hearing from churches and government offices all over the country that also needed help to reach the girls in their own areas.

One pastor whom we knew very well because his church was near our dairy farm told us about the trafficking problem that existed even out in the rural areas. We also had a food storage facility near there—in the middle of nowhere. I asked the pastor if he could get some of the girls to come there that night, because we were going to transform the facility into a block party just for them, complete with dinner. We told him that we were going to treat them as queens for the day. He agreed and spoke to the local mayor to get his permission. The mayor loved the idea. We then talked to a local restaurant and hired them to cater the event. All this came together in one afternoon with an idea we had at about 2:00 p.m.

About 6:00 p.m., the pastor showed up with eighty-five girls. "Where did these girls come from?" I asked.

"These were just the ones I could reach in an afternoon!" he replied. "There are many more." Throughout the night, the girls laughed and ate—and through translators, we heard the same tragic stories that we have heard for years. Many had been abused as children. Many had parents who died. Somewhere in that process, traffickers found them and enslaved them in this system. No matter how many times we've heard it, it crushes us beyond description.

Though I didn't speak their language, there was such a spirit of joy and gratitude that permeated the block party that night. It was one of the best times I have ever had in my entire life. We shared our lives with the girls and they shared their lives with us—and there was a sense of hope that emerged for lives different than the ones they thought they were trapped in forever.

They caught their first glimpse of the glorious unknown.

The block party eventually spawned the launch of a new Refuge home in that area. Even so, there truly is nothing in this world like our Mercy Chapel graduations. When we bought the facility that we now use, it was a brothel—a place where girls were exploited and abused. A church in Atlanta gave the money for us to use to rescue girls, and you can probably imagine their reaction when they heard we had used their donations to buy a brothel. They loved the idea! After all, we converted it into a place where girls are redeemed, healed, and equipped to live the kinds of lives God intended for them. Across all of our programs, thousands of girls have been rescued and have walked away from the tragic lives that they once could never conceive of leaving.

When it's time for their graduation at Mercy Chapel, we make it a major production, just like graduations here in the States. We rent caps and gowns and invite everyone in the area to come celebrate at a ceremony followed by a huge reception with a full-course meal. We pull out all the stops because this moment of transformation is worth celebrating—and the celebration itself serves dual purposes.

We give out special awards throughout the night, honoring the top students in each of the apprenticeship programs: sewing, hairdressing, and the like. One year, we showcased several of our students' fashion designs, which included wedding dresses and evening gowns that were beyond impressive. Our graduates feel the level of love and pride we have for them and the work they have put in.

I know that it might be easy to think: who wouldn't jump at the chance to get out of the red-light district and all that it entails? The truth is, like many people in our own culture, making a major life change from the only thing you've ever known comes with a level of fear and anxiety beyond logic. We often choose the bad that we know and can predict versus the possible good that we have never known that feels terrifyingly unpredictable. It takes a lot of courage for these girls to defy the only thing they've known and launch into the unknown.

This is the other reason for our celebration: to keep chipping away at what is unknown and scary so other girls can see that it is a path they too can be courageous enough to choose. This is why we invite more than 500 girls from the red-light district to watch from the crowd as their friends graduate from the Mercy Chapel program. They come thinking this is something they could never do, but they leave knowing that this is something possible not just for their friends, but also for them. The event helps the unknown become less scary and more glorious. For a day, they see real girls just like them who have found hope—and again, hope is contagious.

Girls who have previously graduated from the program help prepare and serve the meals to the new graduates and our guests still stuck in the red-light district. This means more than 600 people are involved—talk about pandemonium! It is certainly that, in all its glory. These interactions are so very intimate and personal—one person now in freedom selflessly and graciously serving another person still stuck in bondage. It is a beautiful thing, a God thing.

At the end, we have former and current graduates share their stories of redemption. They share their own versions of the familiar narratives of abuse, abandonment, poverty, and exploitation. They share what they were feeling the first time they considered taking a step towards freedom. Their boldness and willingness to talk about these things to a huge group of people is mind-blowing to the listeners, many of whom truly believe they have no worth, no choices, and no voice. One girl said that every day, she knew she would be someone's toilet—these are the kinds of stories being shared all around this graduation event.

At the end, I stand up and give a brief invitation for anyone who wants to take their own first steps towards freedom. I share the same message I have shared with so many in their own individual shacks: God sees what you're going through, God loves you and has a better plan for your life. He has sent people from all sides of the world to help you pursue this better life.

During one graduation alone, we had more than 150 girls from the red-light district become a part of the Mercy Chapel program. Technically, we were only equipped for one hundred girls per session—I guess it was just another one of God's reminders not to ask Him for or believe for too little.

These kinds of events and responses are so encouraging, but they are still not even scratching the surface of the full problem. We cannot stop and rest on our laurels—there are still tens of thousands of girls in East Africa alone enslaved in forced prostitution. Let me pause here to ask you to think of them and to consider what you might be able to do to help. Crisis Aid is dedicated to rescuing as many of them as possible and not stopping until none remain who are being abused and exploited. We're believing God for the biggest of outcomes and working as if He is going to keep providing all we need to make it happen.

We'd love for you to join us in this cause because it really isn't just about the huge statistics—it is about each individual girl. In fact, every time I listen to the hundreds of testimonies from girls once enslaved who are now free and fully alive, I always think back to the first two girls God ever led me to talk to.

I think back to Zuri and Melasech.

Weddings and Funerals

Zuri's life was completely changed by the love of Christ. She was able to begin healing from the life she had been thrust into. This is not to say that there aren't still very real scars or that this has been easy. It is not always easy, but God has been faithful to not only walk with her Himself, but also to send others who were willing to walk with her as she engaged her new life.

My wife and I are the ones who experienced the most honored walk of all—we walked her down the aisle. Actually, we walked the first three girls we rescued down the aisle in the same wedding ceremony. They all got married at the same time to honorable young men.

Today, all three of these young women work full-time for Crisis Aid, helping to rescue other girls like themselves—young women whose lives have immeasurable value hidden in the back alleys and makeshift shacks where sewage runs in the streets and each day feels like a nightmare. They are proof that God sees them and is about the business of rescuing them.

Every time we have a graduating class at Mercy Chapel, I also think of Melasech. When we rescued her out of the red-light district, we administered medical care, which consisted of several screening processes. Unfortunately, Melasech tested positive for HIV. In 2007 in this area of the world, AIDS was almost certainly a death sentence. We were fortunate that one of our country directors is also an ob-gyn who specialized in HIV and AIDS treatments, so we were able to immediately start Melasech on a medicinal regimen to try to slow the effects of the virus.

Time went on and Melasech did pretty well, all things considered. She had bouts here and there, but always bounced back. We often came to East Africa, and seeing these girls so many times made them become like beloved daughters. It was a special connection that only God could have fostered. When they call us "Mom" and "Dad," it brings indescribable joy to our hearts.

One day when I was back home, the phone rang. It was the director. Melasech had become sick again, but this time it didn't look like she was going to be able to pull through. I told him that I would drop everything and head that way—and I asked him how much time we had. He said that we didn't have much.

I began booking my flights as quickly as possible, but Africa is not exactly a hop, skip, and a jump away. The doctor called again and said that she was deteriorating rapidly. I asked if I could talk to her on the phone.

We had the sweetest conversation imaginable—these were the last words between a daughter and a father. I told her that I was trying to get there. She understood. She knew that she was dying, that I loved her, and that she loved me—she made sure that I understood that she knew all these things. Melasech told me I was the only father she had known. She knew what was most important. She knew we would never speak again this side of heaven. I, however, hung up fully expecting to have a few more days with her before she died.

The next morning, I was preparing to leave when the doctor called. Melasech had passed away. I was devastated. I asked the doctor if they could hold off the funeral, and he said that since they didn't embalm their dead, it was their custom to bury them on the very same day they died.

There was nothing he could do. I was going to miss the funeral. I asked the doctor to please tell her story and ask anyone at the funeral who wanted to meet the Jesus who rescued Melasech to come and pray with him. He agreed.

After we hung up, the news that I had missed seeing her one last time crushed me. I had lost a daughter. I felt that I let her down by not getting there before she went home to heaven. I walked into my backyard and I sobbed uncontrollably.

I wasn't there to see it, but that afternoon, more than 150 girls from the red-light district attended Melasech's funeral. The doctor shared the gospel, and many responded to Christ. Many also heard the story of hope that God's love wanted to free them from their slavery.

Back then, the terms "human trafficking" or "sex trafficking" were not yet predominant. There were only a few organizations in the world that we knew of dealing with this issue. When I share in churches about our work with the girls in the red-light

> NO MATTER HOW BAD WE THINK WE ARE OR SOMEONE ELSE MIGHT BE, GOD'S LOVE EXTENDS TO EVERY SINGLE PERSON.

districts, I always talk about Zuri and the power of her one yes. It may have seemed so small in the moment, but on the grand scale of God's inner workings, it triggered so many other yeses from so many other girls who would be rescued out of the red-light district—and also rescued for eternity.

I also always share about Melasech and the fact that even in her death, God used her life to speak hope and salvation to so many. Her picture remains on my desk as I write this. I am still moved to tears by her story—and we still miss her so very much. Yet her life and death were not wasted. Not only did God redeem her and restore her to full life into eternity—I believe that through Zuri and Melasech and those who followed in their brave footsteps, God has let us be a part of helping to birth awareness and change around the world in the growing arena of sex trafficking. Today, these young women run 80 percent of our program to rescue others from the red-light district. They show us why it is important to keep asking better questions and to be willing to say yes.

Dealing with the Hate of It All

It is easy to hate the pimps in the red-light districts for what they are doing. This is a complex situation that requires some sensitivity to address because absolutely, unequivocally, there is no excuse for the heinous and criminal acts they are perpetrating upon these girls. At first, I wanted to kill them and rescue the girls by force. I wanted to hire local motor-cycle hit squads to take them out one by one.

I'm not proud of it, but as a dad to a daughter, can you blame me? Imagine if this were own your daughter, niece, or sister. How would you feel toward the people who are enslaving them to this literal hell? God had to change my heart on this issue, and He had just the thing to do it. Let's leave East Africa for a moment and head to Cambodia.

We had opened a home in Cambodia that housed twenty-seven girls who ranged in age from four years old to twelve. The police had rescued them from a brothel and brought them to us. Their situation had been an unthinkable atrocity, especially for girls this young. We had partnered with an incredible group of local church leaders to continue the work there.

One day, one of these workers told me a story about two of the girls—sisters—who were six and eight years old. They lived in the brothel because their mother sold them to the owners for $300. She knew full well what would become of them there, but she did it anyway.

We had made a connection with the girls' grandmother and heard that the mother was currently staying at her house. I thought to myself, *I've never met someone who would be willing to sell her own children.* For whatever reason, I felt compelled to meet in person someone who was so evil. I asked our friends if they would take us. They called the grandmother, and she agreed to let us come.

It was extremely humid, so by the time we reached her house, I was drenched in sweat. The grandmother was a Christian, and she went on and on thanking us for what we had done for the girls. She was kind and gracious. On the other hand, her daughter—the girls' mother—couldn't sit still long enough to talk to us. She was shiftless, coming and going in and out of the room while smoking cigarettes or doing anything she could to stay in nervous motion.

Finally, she agreed to sit down and talk with us. At first, it was small talk, but as the conversation persisted, I heard God's voice in my heart: "If you could look into her heart, what do you think you would see?"

In my mind, I instinctively answered, "I would see blackness and pure evil." After all, she had done the unspeakable by selling her own children into sexual slavery. Then God spoke again.

"Pat, that's how your heart looked before you came to me."

His words unhinged something in me. It was like I was back in that church the day I first heard God's voice. I began sobbing uncontrollably. Once again, I felt like I was crazy and I was embarrassed, but I couldn't stop. The waves of emotion just kept coming. The woman stopped talking and just stared at me with the strangest expression.

No one had said anything.

Suddenly, the interpreter began crying as well. A few minutes later, the grandmother began crying as well. I know how it sounds, but trust me, it was way weirder than you think. If it wasn't true and so important, I would skip telling it.

The mother sat there looking at all of us carrying on like insane people, and she began to become increasingly agitated, as if something was building up inside of her. I'm not sure how long we cried, but all of a sudden, the mother's body language changed and instead of being agitated, she also began to cry. Something changed, and it didn't happen because I had convinced the woman how bad her sin was. She already knew. Something happened because God wanted to convince me that no one in this world, no matter who they are, needs grace more than I do. No matter how bad we think we are or someone else might be, God's love extends to every single person.

When we all settled down, we led the children's mother to Christ that day. When we got back to the girls' home, the two little sisters came running up to us and jumped into my arms. I didn't understand what they were saying, but they kept kissing me on the cheek and hugging my neck. The interpreter finally calmed them down enough to translate. She had called on the way home to tell them what happened with their mother, and they were overjoyed. They had been praying for their mom ever since they came into the home, and God had heard their prayers. He had removed the hatred from their hearts, and from mine as well.

God taught me that day that if you allow hatred in your heart, you will not be effective in His work. If by God's strength you refuse to let the hatred overtake you, you will be able to love people on a level that you've never been able to before because that which wants to take the place of God's love in your heart will no longer be in control. A love for God and a hatred for humanity cannot coexist within us. "Human anger does not produce the righteousness God desires" (James 1:20).

God knew that I would need this lesson for my work in East Africa. He wanted me to love the pimps just as much as I loved the girls, which seems crazy, but in the context of grace, makes perfect Kingdom sense. Yes, I want them to be stopped and to face the consequences of their actions, but I no longer want them to be destroyed for what they've done.

I tell Christians in churches where I speak to not let any kind of hate in at all. Hate just becomes a foothold for the enemy. You, whether you are a pastor or a prodigal, do not need any less grace today than an East African pimp does. If this offends you, welcome to the work of the gospel—it breaks down what we think we've built up so that Christ can build something else in us that actually stands.

The earthly consequences for my sin may not be the same as someone trafficking other humans, but my dire need for Jesus' grace is identical. If you instinctively believe that there is someone on this planet who needs grace more than you, this is an indicator that you may not fully perceive the depth of your separation from God without Christ's intervention.

It also means that you will have trouble being used by God to love those who you think deserve His love less than you.

This came to bear one night when I was in the red-light district. It was an unusually dark night because the electricity was out. Along with the moon moving in and out of the clouds, only the candles in the girls' rooms provided light. We had to watch where we stepped. While we were talking with some girls, a policeman approached me and told me that I needed to leave right then because a group of pimps standing near us had been overhead threatening to kill me. Instead of walking away, I felt compelled to walk right up to them. But it was not to fight, not anymore.

The pimps looked stunned to see me, but I felt resolute. "Let me tell you guys something," I said, "God sees what you're doing to these girls, and He's disgusted with it. This is wrong. But listen, He also sees you and where you are. He has a better plan for your lives as well."

Some of them spoke English and others did not, but I think my message got through to them. Instead of killing me (which is always a real possibility), three of them walked away and four of them stayed so that I could pray with them as they gave their lives to Christ that night. We didn't have a lot of opportunity to follow up with them, but I later found out that they left the red-light district and never came back. We had the same thing happen with some pimps in Haiti: they left their horrible work and never returned to it.

From a justice standpoint, I understand that this doesn't restore what has been taken away from the girls, and I'm not acting as if it does. I only mean that God really does love the pimps as much as He loves the sex slaves—and as much as He loves you. Let this offend you every day as it changes you into someone you could never be on your own: a new creation—not made new by your own efforts, but by the grace of One who sees you right where you are, no matter where that may be.

BUT NO MATTER WHAT, IT ALL MUST BEGIN WITH LOVE, OR ELSE IT'S ALL A WASTE OF TIME.

The issues of trafficking in these areas are systemic in nature, and the love of God needs to be brought into the entire equation. Jesus didn't love His disciples more than he loved the Pharisees. He didn't like what the Pharisees were doing to the people—it made Him angry. This makes us angry as well, and we are doing something to respond.

But no matter what, it all must begin with love, or else it's all a waste of time.

NINE

When Disaster Strikes

Indonesia, Pakistan, and Haiti

Much of our time in Sudan, Afghanistan, and East Africa centered upon helping refugees who were fleeing war zones or meeting the needs of people stuck in cycles of famine, poverty, or slavery. However, many times over the years we have responded to the needs of people devastated by natural disasters and the terrifying aftermath.

One of our first disaster relief efforts came in 2004, when three ninety-foot tsunami waves decimated the people and lands of Indonesia and its surrounding population the day after Christmas. All told, about 230,000 people lost their lives. It was a horrific disaster on an almost incalculable scale.

I had a few contacts in the area from a trip I had taken there in the 1990s while investigating Christian persecution. The missionaries I knew connected us with a church that was about fifty miles from the epicenter of the damage, which was exactly where we were trying to get to. In addition to the incredible logistical challenges caused by the tsunami itself, we missed one of our connecting flights because of a snowstorm in Minneapolis. In all, it took us six days to get to Indonesia.

We landed in Medan, the capital of Indonesia's North Sumatra province, where the UN was headquartering all their relief operations. We arrived late in the evening and got up early to attend a UN–hosted meeting for relief organizations. Over the years, we have learned that the first couple of weeks after a disaster are the most critical in terms of saving lives. One of the reasons for this is the amount of time it takes the UN and other large global organizations to organize and set up their infrastructure, as well as their supply and distribution processes. Managing these amid geopolitical boundaries, treaties, and international customs disputes is a logistical and political nightmare of red tape, but it has to be done.

Yet in the meantime, people are suffering greatly. This is why organizations like Crisis Aid are so important. While global organizations are sorting out their bureaucracy, we can be one of the first on the ground to help people at the epicenter of the disaster.

In this case, we learned that it would be two weeks before the UN would be able to begin distributing aid to the people living in the areas destroyed by the tsunami. There were also unique challenges related to distribution because all the telecommunications and electricity in the area were down, and all the major roads were damaged. When we left the meeting, we knew that there were a lot of people out there who could not survive for two weeks without aid. We decided to follow God's lead and get to work immediately, seeing where He would take us.

Since more than a hundred miles of roads were impassable in all directions, we were thrilled to find out that a local church had a wealthy member who owned a helicopter. It was the only way we could survey the damage and plan our next steps. We call this kind of mission a "recce," which is short for reconnaissance. I remember thinking how crazy it was that the UN couldn't yet get into these areas to help, but God had put us right there in the middle of it all.

We were never able to land, but we did gather enough data to begin formulating a plan. We had to secure trucks that could transport whatever aid we gathered. Within three or four days, a couple of the roads had been reopened with makeshift bridges, which meant that our trucks could reach a few of the areas within the disaster zone. By that time, we had accumulated three or four tons of food and supplies and had begun taking it to the people we could reach with the trucks.

However, we were still struggling to find a system to reach the people who lived deep in the affected areas. That's when I met a guy from an organization called Missionary Aviation Fellowship, or MAF. He had flown over the wreckage even farther than we had gone in the helicopter and had seen what he believed to be the actual epicenter of the damage on the other side of a mountain range. I asked him if he could show me and he agreed, though he made it clear that we might not be able to land.

We circled the area he had mentioned and found what looked like a big enough strip of an old road to barely land the one-engine Cessna plane. As he came in for a landing, I could tell that we were going to be cutting it close with the amount of "runway" below us. He dropped the plane down as if it was falling straight to the ground—I like to say that we crashed, but that's only the way it felt. He slammed on the brakes and the plane stopped literally a few feet from the end of the road.

We were on the ground, but it was so close that we literally had to get out and pick up the tail of the plane to spin it around and back it up to the very edge of the road in hopes that we would have enough runway to take off again. Since you're reading this story, you already know that it worked, but barely.

Once on the ground, survivors of the tsunami began coming out of the jungle to meet us. They told us all that had happened to them that fateful morning. Out of nowhere, the ocean seemed to disappear—it just went backwards, leaving nothing but sand with fish flopping around almost as far as the eye could see. People ran out to gather up the fish, trying to figure out what was happening. Then, suddenly, they saw the first of three huge waves in the distance. It was too late for many of them. We were standing where the waves had their biggest impact. The waves were ninety feet high, which seems almost impossible to imagine. We were standing in a place where the ground had been completely washed away, leaving nothing but a crater. It was just gone. The level ground was about twenty or thirty feet above us. There was a tall coconut tree that had survived on the level ground, and as I looked up, I saw debris in its branches. Sure enough, this was probably at least eighty feet above where I was standing.

"My God," I whispered.

We were able to ascertain their greatest immediate needs so our new pilot friend could begin ferrying in loads of medical supplies and food for them. I don't remember "preaching" the gospel or anything like that. We just shared who we were and why we were there to help. They were gracious towards us in response.

WHEN PEOPLE LOVE ONE ANOTHER, THERE IS JOY EVEN IN DISASTER. THIS DOESN'T MINIMALIZE PEOPLE'S PAIN; RATHER, IT DEMONSTRATES THAT GOD IS PRESENT AND ACTIVE IN IT.

We spent two years coming and going to help with the relief efforts, building new relationships along the way that would last a lifetime. We actually had fun with our new friends, even though the disaster around us was immeasurable. When people love one another, there is joy even in disaster. This doesn't minimalize people's pain; rather, it demonstrates that God is present and active in it.

When we first decided to go, which was only a few days after the tsunami, we had less than $10,000. We reached out to our friends and supporters to let them know that we were going to do something, and within a few weeks, more than $100,000 had come in. We were able to not only offer medical supplies and food, but over time, we rebuilt more than twenty homes. Many other individuals and organizations showed up and chipped in, both locally and from around the world. We were just amazed at how much God did—and that He let us be a part of the work.

This project helped us establish the framework for our future process of responding to natural disasters. We always try to partner with local churches because they not only know the area and people affected by the disaster, but they will be there with them after we leave. Crisis Aid is not just about doing our own thing, but rather we exist to equip the local church to help the people around them not just through words, but also through real action.

Earthquake in Pakistan

In 2005, an earthquake that registered 7.6 on the Richter scale rattled Pakistan and Afghanistan. This was another moment of divine appointment for us because we were already working in the area. I immediately reached out to my friend, Shahbaz, and he confirmed the reports of the vast devastation and began helping us reach out to our local contacts to gather supplies and aid for a response.

Within a few days, I was on a flight from St. Louis to Pakistan via a stop in London. I remember watching the news reports on the tiny monitors on the backs of the plane seats and hearing them say that there were virtually no trucks, no cars, no food, no tents, no plastic, no blankets—no supplies to be found anywhere in the country. The UN had gathered what few supplies there were for their relief efforts. I thought to myself, *I should just get off this plane and go home.* But something inside reminded me that I rarely know how things will work out when I take the first step, so I should just keep going.

When I landed and made my way into the city, I began securing supplies and trucks to deliver them. Shahbaz and our mutual contacts assisted in the process. We had told them what we wanted to do—to provide food, water, and shelter for people in the worst areas of damage. So even as the biggest story circulating around the world was that nothing was available, through our work and the work of our partners, God helped us track down what we needed.

We made our way to the city near the epicenter of the quake. It was in the Himalayan Mountains, the largest mountain range in the world. What I saw in those mountains was unlike anything I had seen in all my travels. Whole sides of mountains were just smashed in as if someone had punched them with a giant fist. It was absolute destruction in an area where tens of thousands of people lived. About 100,000 people died in the earthquake, including more than 19,000 children, most of whom lost their lives when school buildings collapsed upon them.

I had witnessed firsthand the devastation of the tsunami, but from a pure visual perspective, in and around those mountains the destruction was on another level, perhaps because of the nature of the geography. Sections of the most rugged mountain range in the world had been crumpled up like a piece of paper. It was indescribable.

We sprang into action to help and began distributing multiple tons of food and aid to the people most deeply affected, including materials to build shelters—plastic sheeting and the like. As we worked, one of the most significant things that happened occurred out of the blue. We somehow ended up being connected to a high-ranking officer in the Pakistani military. He was the person responsible for all the disaster assistance from the Pakistan government.

They had helicopters and knew of many people and villages beyond the city who were in dire straits. The problem was that they had run out of supplies and didn't have immediate access to more. He told me that things were a lot worse in these areas than people realized. Many people had died, and many others were trying to survive by huddling together the best they could on the sides of the mountains. He knew what was happening, but the military had nothing to take them.

That's when I asked another strange (and perhaps better) question of the Pakistani military leader: "Do you want to work together?"

For the next week or so, Crisis Aid ferried food and supplies through the Pakistani military to places thought impossible to reach. When the world thought there was no aid and no chance to deliver it, God provided everything we needed and more. As has happened many times over the years, this was another moment when we, as Christians, were able to work in harmony with Muslims. They knew who we were, and we knew who they were. The truth is, they were thrilled to have our assistance—and we were thrilled to be able to show them the love that Christ has shown us.

Some time later, the Pakistani military wrote us a letter of gratitude. In it, they acknowledged that during the distributions we had won the hearts of the people and "this gesture of love will strengthen the bonds between our two countries." Ours was an unlikely partnership, but God had plans bigger than our own—and when He sends you to do something, you just never know where your path might lead and whose path yours might cross in the process.

While in the city where we were working, I joked with Shahbaz that it would be crazy if they were to find Osama Bin Laden in that area. We laughed it off at the time. Years later, this was exactly where they found him, though I doubt he was there at the same time as us.

Earthquake in Haiti

In 2010, tragedy struck again, this time in one of the poorest nations of the world. A 7.0 earthquake rocked the island nation of Haiti. Amid the chaos, the exact numbers are disputed, but somewhere between 250,000 and 300,000 people lost their lives.

We had just arrived at a condominium in Florida where our daughter lived. We walked in the door with our suitcases to see the news headline on the television: "Earthquake Destroys Haiti!" I felt the little switch flip within me—I knew God wanted me to go. Five minutes later, a pastor from Victory Church in Atlanta called my cell phone. She asked if we were going and what they could do to help.

We were supposed to be with our daughter for two weeks, so I questioned whether we should go. I said, "I tell you what, it would take at least $20,000 for us to even be able to take an exploratory trip. You know?"

"I'll call you back," she said.

A few minutes later, she called back. "You've got the $20,000."

And that was that. The church's missions pastor, who would turn out to become a good friend through this process, had some contacts in Haiti through which we began making inquiries. Flights into Haiti were very difficult to secure, and we were being told that anyone who came to help should bring body bags. I remember asking, "Body bags? Where do you buy those?"

The next several days were spent making constant calls and inquiries, just trying to gain access to the country while also trying to get emergency aid and supplies purchased and on their way to the island. It was a logistical nightmare, but we persisted. Our best bet was to see what we could personally take into the country—if we could get access.

God opened up a door, and we were told we would be allowed to come, but there was still so much we didn't know. Just before we were about to leave from Miami, we received a call from the *St. Louis Post-Dispatch* newspaper. They wanted to know what we were doing in response to the earthquake and if they could send a reporter and a photographer to tag along. We figured that they wanted to report on the earthquake, but since no one was being allowed into the country, they could travel with us and then we would go our separate ways. We knew that this was an important story, so we said yes.

It took us an extra four days in Miami to get them added to our team so they could be granted entry, but it finally came through and we boarded a plane for the short flight to what might as well have been another planet. We were meeting with an organization on the ground that assured us they would have everything ready for us when we arrived. They were working with the UN to provide a security force that would accompany us from the moment we touched down throughout all our travels to various distribution sites. Relief work in moments of extreme disaster can quickly become very dangerous because people are desperate.

As we waited in the Miami airport to board our flight, I told the reporters, "Good luck! I look forward to reading your stories."

They looked at me in bewilderment. "Mr. Bradley, we're here to cover you."

"What?"

"Yeah, you're the story. This is a human interest story, and we're covering Crisis Aid, but specifically, we're here to shadow you."

This was not good news. This was a level of pressure that I didn't need and that could distract us from the work at hand, but there was no talking them out of it. We were walking into more unknowns than I had ever experienced, and now we had a team of journalists chronicling our every move.

This was not going in the right direction—and it was about to get worse.

As soon as we landed on the airstrip in Port-au-Prince, the runway lights went out. We taxied over and the pilot shut down the plane. The crew left, and we found ourselves standing outside on the tarmac of the airport. Something was terribly wrong. Where were our vehicles? Where was our security? No one showed up.

We spent the night sleeping in the luggage carts they used to load the planes.

The next day, someone from the organization that promised to meet us finally showed up and took us to a meeting, where they presented all their plans. When we left the meeting, I turned to the reporters and said, "We're done. These guys mean well, but they're never going to be able to get anything off the ground and running." And it turned out, they never did. We decided to just figure things out on our own—to follow the Lord's leading and see where He took us.

Somehow, we managed to secure the courtyard of a church where we could sleep in tents at night. The temperature and humidity made it absolutely miserable, and we spent all day and all night covered in sweat. A few days later, we met an American missionary who was leaving the country and had been staying at a hotel built by Germans. Since the Germans had built it according to their stricter codes, it had sustained some damage, but had mostly survived the earthquake intact.

He offered us the room he was vacating—and after four days of miserable conditions, we were grateful to take it and to finally have a place from which to begin planning our operations. Oh yeah, and it had air-conditioning and showers, which were the best things that had happened to us so far on this trip. I was mortified because the reporters were seeing nothing but a series of mishaps and shortfalls. We hadn't helped a single person yet. We needed God to get us to those who needed help—and we needed it now.

Another missionary told us about Léogâne, the city located at the epicenter of the earthquake. It had experienced sheer destruction, and no relief efforts had reached the people who lived there. That was what we needed to hear—that was where we needed to go. When we arrived, his descriptions proved accurate. Everything was leveled. It was utter mass destruction. This was about eight days after the earthquake, and when we pulled up, we found people living in little camps, struggling to pool together enough food and supplies to survive another day.

This was not our usual process. With very few contacts in the area, we were flying blind. We pulled into one of the camps and immediately encountered the difficulty of the language barrier—and we had no translators. God provided, as usual. A woman named Nunu approached us with just what we needed the most at that moment: she spoke English. She caught us up on the situation, including what the people there were lacking and what they were waiting on the UN to bring. For whatever reason, the UN was not distributing anything to them. We said that we would go talk with the UN representatives and see what we could do to help.

The UN security forces for that area were from the Sri Lankan military—they were in charge. We went in to meet with the Sri Lankan commander and explained that we were a USAID–approved organization, which is usually a door opener around the world because it lets anyone know that we have the qualifications and experience to distribute aid in any number of disaster scenarios.

We asked them about the supplies that we knew they had and asked if we could help distribute them. To our surprise, they curtly said no. We asked them when they were planning to distribute the aid. They said there was nothing planned. This went on for about twenty minutes, and I quickly concluded that this tactic wasn't going to work.

I was angry. The reporter and photographer who were with us had now become friends, and as we walked out of the meeting, they asked me what I was thinking about what had just happened. I answered them with some very choice words not suitable for children. "You want us to write that?" they asked.

"No!" I huffed. "You just asked me what I thought!" I was frustrated over the whole situation, and it felt like there was nothing we could do. This was a disaster within a disaster.

As we walked away, a major from the US Marines walked past us on his way to speak with the Sri Lankans. I was seeing too much red to even notice him. When we got into our car, the driver said, "Mr. Pat, did you see that marine walk in?"

"Yeah, I saw him. What about him?"

"Maybe you should go talk to him."

"Why?" I wanted to leave this frustrating situation behind. But the driver kept insisting that I try to speak with the marine, so I finally relented and got out of the car to walk back towards the door. Sure enough, in a few minutes the major emerged and I could tell that he was even angrier than I was. I stopped him and explained who I was and what Crisis Aid was here to do. When he heard that we were USAID–approved and that we had provided aid after the Indonesian tsunami and the Pakistani earthquake, he perked up. Little did I know that God had just put me direcly in the path of the only guy in Haiti who could help us at that moment in time. I'm not sure how our driver knew—maybe God knew that I was too angry to listen.

We began comparing notes, and within a few minutes, we understood the collective problem. He said that the US Marines had been flying supplies from Navy ships into the area for eight days, dropping them by helicopter into a huge clearing not too far from where we were. Curiously, the US Congress had approved the delivery of the aid but had prohibited the US military from distributing it to the locals. The agreement with the UN was that the Sri Lankans were supposed to distribute it, but they were refusing. The major's hands were tied, just like ours.

"So you're telling me that you have tons upon tons of

supplies out in a field near here just sitting there with no one able or willing to distribute it?" I asked.

"Pat, I'm telling you that we have armed marines guarding the perimeter of the aid and that the locals are standing around begging for food and supplies—and we can't give it to them." He was disgusted, but he had his orders.

He took us to the field, and sure enough, it was like a scene from *The Hunger Games*. People were gathered around just looking at food, water, blankets, and medical aid while armed soldiers prevented them from getting it. These marines had been transferred here from Iraq and were decked out in full gear from head to toe. They were sweating so badly in the blistering heat that they had to take two-hour shifts just to avoid heat stroke. Things were getting tense, on the verge of a riot. Seemingly, nothing could be done.

Which is why God put us right there in that exact moment.

Knowing our credentials, the major offered us the job of distributing the aid. We accepted. What had been almost a week-long fiasco suddenly materialized into just the scenario to help those most in need. God knew what He was doing, even when I was busy arguing with the Sri Lankans.

We began by speaking to the sergeant in charge of logistics. He was glad we were there, but he said that unless we could secure trucks, this wasn't going to work. It was a multi-acre field piled high with tons upon tons of supplies. We weren't going to be able to just start unloading by hand or walking it inland on our backs. He was also angry with the Sri Lankans. "We are supposed to give it to them, but they aren't coming, so screw 'em!"

His words, not mine.

"We'll be back here tomorrow at 8:00 a.m. with two trucks." As I said the words, our team looked at me in puzzlement. They knew that finding trucks in a disaster zone like this was a virtual impossibility. We had already been trying for days, with no success, on the off chance that we might get to distribute food at some point. As we were driving back to our hotel, we came upon a big truck pulled over on the side of the road. I got out to talk to the driver. He must have thought we were crazy, but we told him what we needed—and then we agreed on a per-day rate. We now had a truck.

We got back in the car and went a few more miles, and we came upon another truck pulled over. Same story. We stopped. We talked. We paid. He agreed. Within an hour of my Hail Mary, we had secured two trucks and were ready to go.

The next morning, we pulled up to the Marine camp with two huge trucks and their jaws dropped. We got to work, and within a few days of laboring together, we had become fast friends with most of the soldiers. They helped us load things up and we began driving the aid to the surrounding villages, doing what we had come there to do. There was not much of a church presence in this area, so we worked with local contacts we were making on the ground as we went.

In the meantime, the Canadian military had arrived and was tasked with beginning to rebuild essential public buildings like orphanages and schools. They heard about what we were doing and asked for a meeting. They were also facing diplomatic restrictions on what they could do, so they vetted us and offered us the job of taking the lead on the rebuilding work. The agreement was that we would have complete autonomy in using their supplies and their soldiers, sending them to do whatever needed to be done. We said yes and immediately began rebuilding orphanages and schools all over the area with the help of the Canadian military.

The first orphanage we rebuilt actually found us, in a way. One day we heard what sounded like the voices of angels singing together. When we followed the sound, we discovered that it was coming from the mouths of children outside the rubble of their orphanage, which lay in complete disarray, destroyed by the earthquake. Miraculously, no children from the orphanage were killed in the earthquake. We found that first orphanage to begin rebuilding through the beautiful voices of the ones we were there to love and serve.

A week or so into our process, our Marine friends told us that more soldiers and equipment were arriving every day on Navy and Coast Guard ships, but they were just sitting anchored out in the bay because their hands were tied with the same red tape that had stopped the Marines. The Marines informed the Navy and Coast Guard commanders: "If you don't give the aid to Crisis Aid to distribute, you might as well throw it in the bay." They listened, and soon we were working with them as well.

We had been there for three weeks, and in that short time, the US Navy, the US Marines, the US Coast Guard, the Canadian Navy, and the Canadian Army were all basically working for Crisis Aid. It was so cool! I remember watching huge helicopter gunships loaded with food and supplies hovering over the fields. They would land, and the marines would off-load the supplies onto our trucks. Before they could take off, two more were already waiting to land.

I know that God has no limits, but this felt like He was spoiling us just for fun.

I KNOW THAT GOD HAS NO LIMITS, BUT THIS FELT LIKE HE WAS SPOILING US JUST FOR FUN.

Toward the end of our time on the island, we found a store that was selling cold beer. We bought a few cases and delivered them to our Marine friends as a gesture of gratitude. This exchange went on for several weeks. They gave us so much food and supplies and we just wanted to thank them the best we could—and a cold beer in Haiti was just the trick! About a week later, the Marine major caught up with me and expressed his gratitude for all that we had done to help. He also informed me that technically, since they were on active duty twenty-four hours a day in this disaster zone, his soldiers were not allowed to drink. "Do you think I would do something so childish as get cold beer for your Marines?" I asked.

He smiled slyly—and though I have no reason to doubt him, let's just say that they never returned the beer.

I was then invited to a meeting with a five-star general. He was a member of the Joint Chiefs of Staff and was in charge of logistics for the entire US military. He said that his men had informed him of what we had done, so he presented us with a military coin, a very rare honor for civilians. I was told that fewer than a dozen per year were given to civilians.

All we had really done was just show up.

In the end, we had spent only about $50,000 on our efforts. We had arrived with next to nothing, and though everything went down the toilet for a few days, God redeemed it all. Speaking of redemption, because the military keeps such accurate records, we were able to ascertain that they brought in nearly a million dollars' worth of aid that we distributed, which means that we gave away a million dollars' worth of aid for only $50,000. That is nothing less than a divine return on investment. We were also able to rebuild about seven orphanages and schools in the area.

The *St. Louis Post-Dispatch* had run daily stories about our trip on the front page for about a week. The stories of the people of Haiti were heard, awareness and funds were raised for their cause, and God was glorified in the middle of our insufficiencies. Oh—and the reporter left out the first few days of the trip, including some of my choice words. It was one more thing to be grateful for.

TEN

Soviet Smugglers and American Traffickers

Soviet Union and United States

It's hard to believe that this is our final chapter. I thought it might be a good time to take you back to the beginning—to my first overseas trip. The book *God's Smuggler* by Brother Andrew had deeply affected me, so it made sense for me to get my first taste of overseas ministry by working with the persecuted church. My first trip was filled with awakenings, some of them rude.

I somehow got connected with a missions pastor over a lunch, and he invited me to join him and a few other friends on a trip to the Soviet Union. They were going to do research, and I told them that I wanted to tag along and smuggle in some Bibles and worship tapes. We agreed, though I didn't

243

really know what I was doing. (You're probably thinking, *Sure, Pat, but what else is new?*)

I ended up on a plane with this guy and two other seasoned pastors. They were all ministers who had traveled the world, while I was a recently sober alcoholic who had given his life to Christ only a few years before. But since it was my idea, I was the one tasked with carrying the Bibles and tapes in my suitcase.

We flew from St. Louis to Helsinki, Finland. Then we caught a ferry into the city of Tallinn in the Soviet Union. When we arrived, we stood on the dock waiting to speak with the customs officers—and I wanted to turn back. The other pastors had told me that they would guide me through what to do, but when we got to customs, they all went their own way. I was alone. Angry. Terrified. What in the world had I done?

Somehow, I made it through customs undetected. This was the most terrified I have ever been in my life, even compared to when I have AK-47s pointed at my head.

I felt out of place because they were all men of God, and I was just a normal guy. I was also the guy lugging all the holy contraband. You would think that I would have wanted to get rid of those Bibles as quickly as possible, but even with my intense fear, I didn't feel released by God to give them away. This persisted for about four days.

One night we were in another meeting with Christian leaders. When it ended, a man stood up to leave and I felt

God speak to me that I should give him one of the Bibles, which we had left in the car outside. I spoke with the translator to make sure it was okay, and then I went to the car to get the Bible. I saw the man in the parking lot, and I called out for him, "Hey!" I didn't know his name and I did not speak one syllable of Russian, but still, he turned around and I waved him over.

I held out the Bible to him. When he saw it, he extended both hands, carefully cupping them together as if he was about to hold something extremely delicate and fragile. I saw a drop of water hit the top of the cover of the Bible. When I looked up, he had tears streaming down his face, but his expression was obviously very mixed. I couldn't read him, but I knew that the Bible had either struck a chord or struck a nerve.

After he left, fear and anxiety overtook me, causing me to think that I had majorly screwed up. When I went back inside, I pulled the interpreter aside and shared my fears. He listened to my story and then interrupted, "You didn't offend him. That man you just met was a pastor who had spent twenty-six years in a Siberian prison. He could have been released at any moment if he just would have denied his Christianity, but he never did."

I was speechless.

"You just gave him the first Bible he has ever owned for himself."

This moment. *This* was the exact second that the "hook" of missions was set in me. There are few words to describe what it felt like to be so underqualified and overwhelmed, yet to be used by God to show His love to someone who had suffered so much. To this day, I get goose bumps when I retell the story. Yes, we were part of a church back home that was very missions-focused, which God used to make me willing to come in the first place. I'm grateful for such a church, but it was this moment that put me forever on a new course. There was no going back.

On another night, we attended a secret prayer meeting in a basement in Tallinn. Through the interpreters, we were asked to come pray for the sick people by laying our hands on them. I had never done such a thing before, and it made me uncomfortable, but we did it.

The next day, we were getting ready to leave for Moscow when a man approached me and asked, "Did you hear what happened? The woman you prayed for was a city administrator—an official leader in the Communist government." I was dumbfounded, not knowing how to respond. The man continued. "She was deaf, and after you prayed for her, she was able to hear. Her picture is on the front page of the newspaper." After that, I decided that praying for people was something I should not avoid, no matter who they were.

We boarded our train for an all-night, fourteen-hour ride to Moscow. We would arrive at 7:00 a.m. to meet our contacts.

As a businessman, I was accustomed to things being well planned, so being completely exhausted from the trip and the overnight train ride, I couldn't believe it when nobody showed up to meet us. It was the dead of winter, and the four of us stood there shivering outside at a train station in Moscow.

"So what's the plan, guys?" I asked.

"Not real sure," one of them replied. "We're supposed to meet someone, I think."

"You think?" I was growing more and more irritated.

Just then, the guy we were supposed to meet walked up. We asked him where we were going, and he said the same thing—he hadn't made any real plans. When he said this, I'm not proud of it, but I lost it on all of them. We were standing there exposed and freezing because a bunch of pastors and their own contact hadn't conducted the proper legwork and logistics to make sure everything was lined up.

"So what are we going to do?" I exclaimed.

"I'm not sure," one pastor replied, "but God will lead us where we need to go."

I was still carrying Bibles and tapes—and we had children and wives back home. I just knew that we were going to be arrested, and it was going to be all their fault! They never said anything in response; they just let me stand there and sound off.

The contact, who was going to also serve as our interpreter, finally said that he thought he knew of a place where we could go. A few hours later, we found ourselves at an underground church meeting—with me still seething over the fact that there was no plan. We were probably putting these poor people in danger because they had no idea we were even coming. This was a disaster. We made our way down to the basement where the meeting was taking place. When we opened the door, I was surprised at the number of people there. My surprise was tripled when, through the interpreter, they told us that they had been expecting us. This was before the days of cell phones, so having just lost my cool (to say it mildly) on the train platform, I was confused.

GOD WAS BLOWING UP MY PRECONCEIVED NOTIONS AND PRIDE, SHOWING ME THINGS ABOUT HIS PLANS FOR MY LIFE BEYOND MY WILDEST DREAMS.

"Did you call them or something?" I asked the interpreter.

"No, I did not," he replied.

They went on to tell us that when they came together before their service to pray as usual, God had told them that people from the West would be showing up this morning. God told them that He had sent us, so they should welcome us. Normally a knock at the door would have terrified them, but knowing we were coming, they were able to answer it with confidence. Once again, God was blowing up my preconceived notions and pride, showing me things about His plans for my life beyond my wildest dreams.

We spent several more days in Moscow meeting with believers and seeing the tourist sites. By this time, all the Bibles had been given away, but I still had the worship tapes. I had not gotten rid of them just yet because I didn't feel like I was supposed to. They were Hosanna Integrity tapes recorded in Russian. I had listened to them so much before the trip that though I had no idea what I was saying, I could sing along with them in perfect Russian. My fellow travelers wanted me to hurry up and get rid of the tapes so we wouldn't be caught on our way out.

We left Moscow for the fourteen-hour train ride back to Tallinn, where we had an eight-hour layover before we were to catch the ferry back to Helsinki. During the layover, I felt a sudden urge to start walking. At first, I just sat there, but it kept getting stronger and stronger. Finally, it felt like a voice in my heart said, "Get up and start walking."

"Hey guys, I'm going to take a walk." One of the guys said that he would go with me, just to be safe. Off we went, taking the worship tapes with us and having no clue where we were going. This was before the days of turn-by-turn GPS, but in my heart, it seemed as if I could hear the directions. *Turn here. Now take a left.*

The city was completely foreign to me, so we quickly became lost, but my pastor friend just kept following me, knowing that God was doing something unique. We eventually came upon a long series of identically ugly apartment buildings, obviously built decades earlier in the 1960s, and not for the sake of aesthetics. The directions in my head continued. *This building. Up these stairs.* If this sounds crazy to you, please know that it was doubly so for me.

Knock on this door.

There I stood, in the middle of Soviet Russia, about to knock on a strange door on the last day of my first trip when I was close to coming home safely. A man opened the door almost as quickly as I had knocked on it. Before I could sputter any words in broken Russian, in perfect English, he asked, "Did you bring the worship tapes?" The pastor and I looked at each other in amazement.

"I missed you the first time you were here, but God told me that He would bring you back because He wants me to have the tapes." We gave him the tapes and retraced our steps back to the train station. That was how my first missions trip ended.

I went on the trip upset that things weren't properly planned, but I came home understanding that God's plans are always bigger, better, and more trustworthy than my own. As you now know, it was a lesson I would need a million more times to come.

Maybe you need it too.

Bringing It Home

Most of this book has focused on what God has done in the lives of people overseas, but odds are, you are reading this between calls at your job or in the booth of a coffee shop—and you are doing so in your hometown, *not* abroad. I told you in the beginning not to fixate on these crazy stories as something that only happens to special people. Because this is not about a certain kind of person or a certain exotic place, you can rest assured that God wants to lead you away from doing nothing in your own hometown. He's leading you, right here. Right now.

Why not you, and why not now?

One of the first moments when God brought the game to my own backyard occurred, ironically, while I was in East Africa in 2008. I was still a partner in an ad agency with over 180 employees. When I was overseas, things could get hairy when my email inbox filled up with problems back home. I finally told my team that I would not be checking email when I was out of the country, so to please not send a lot of messages. If there was an emergency, my wife knew how to reach me. Despite my best intentions, I still made the mistake of checking my email one day and there was a message from an assistant at Crisis Aid that read something like this:

WHY NOT YOU, AND WHY NOT NOW?

Hey Pat! Hope you're having a great trip. Quick thing: the FBI called and they want to meet with you when you get home. Thanks!

I immediately called her on the phone. "What is going on?"

Realizing that her email was a little light on details for such a heavy message, she said, "Oh, I think they just want to talk to you about our work with forced prostitution."

I laughed out loud. "Well, you could have said that!"

When I got home, I went to meet with someone who turned out to be a bigwig—one of the FBI leaders over the eastern half of United States. The FBI had begun cracking down on sex trafficking, becoming more and more serious about addressing what was becoming a huge problem in the US. He opened by asking me to tell him a little about myself. I said, "Well, since you're the FBI, you should probably know that I regularly wire money to Afghanistan."

He laughed. "Pat, we not only know that you do, but we have records of the exact amounts and dates. We're the FBI." We both laughed, one of us more nervously than the other. "We know what you're doing over there—and we think it's a great thing."

We chatted a bit more, and then he asked me what I knew about sex trafficking in the United States. "Well, I've heard that a lot of foreign girls are being brought over and forced into slavery," I said.

"You're right," he said, "but do you know about the

American victims?" He went on to enlighten me to the enormous problem right here at home. More than 300,000 American children were at risk of sexual exploitation every year.

I had always called it forced prostitution while working overseas, but he told me they no longer call it that. The reason is simple: In America, when we use the word "prostitution," many people will automatically think there's a degree of participation on the part of the girl or woman being forced into the situation.

These are not prostitutes; these are prisoners. He continued telling me the statistics and how many minors were being affected around the country. It was devastating to hear. When the FBI was able to rescue the minors, their only option was to put them into protective custody, which was basically equivalent to juvenile detention—jail. There were not many other options at that point in time. He said there were only three organizations in the United States that were taking in young American girls rescued from sex trafficking, which equaled to only forty-nine beds across the whole nation. He was sick of putting girls into detention centers to keep them safe. They needed someone new to step up and begin providing a place for these girls who were being rescued.

Once again, I had no idea what I was doing, but I didn't think it was necessary to stop and pray before saying yes.

We had scheduled a forty-five minute meeting. Two-and-a-half hours later, we were still talking. I left and agreed to fly to Washington, D.C., to meet with more FBI officials to keep discussing the problems and possible solutions. These agents were genuinely sick and tired of seeing these girls mistreated while having so few options to help them in the long run. It moved my heart to see their level of empathy and their willingness to act.

They said that they were talking to us because they loved our organization and the way we were conducting ourselves in other areas of the world. They wanted us to help them find more solutions here as well, specifically with our holistic approach to asking better questions, though they didn't say it exactly that way. They weren't allowed to officially ask us to do anything, but they made their case clear enough that the inference was evident. They said that if we were to ever open a home in the D.C. area, every single one of the agents present would volunteer to help the girls who came in.

Honestly, these FBI agents were refusing to do nothing—and it was inspiring. We told them that, unfortunately, the only way we could pull something off was to begin the work out of our home base in St. Louis. With that, our odyssey of working to rescue girls from sex trafficking in the United States was underway.

We immediately began planning and trying to raise funds to open our first home for girls in St. Louis. Honestly, with the statistics and stories we were telling, as well as our connection to the FBI, I thought people would throw money at us, but for more than three years, people seemed to not want to hear about it at all. For whatever reason, Americans seemed to avoid addressing this issue in their own country. Our efforts felt like trying to plow through cement.

We had other financial challenges as well. It costs ten times more money to put a girl in a home here than it does overseas. For the first three years, I said that we wouldn't open the home until we had a full year's worth of operating cash in the account. I temporarily forgot that God had never before waited until I was ready or equipped to start using us. When we couldn't get over the hump, we knew that girls needed help now, so we scrapped our "responsible" plan and got our first home open and running on faith that God would provide.

God is still changing the lives of girls rescued from the sex trade through multiple Refuge Homes, but it is far from enough. The problem continues to grow. We need many more people who will refuse to do nothing about this problem. As

YOU DON'T NEED TO BE QUALIFIED OR RESOURCED— YOU JUST NEED TO GIVE WHAT YOU HAVE OF YOURSELF AND GOD WILL MAKE GOOD ON THE INVESTMENT

my story proves, you don't need to be qualified or resourced—you just need to give what you have of yourself and God will make good on the investment in ways you never dreamed, mainly because they are impossible.

Restoring Dignity at Home

Our other main project at home in St. Louis involved feeding hungry people in our own backyard. We have sponsored a feeding program for the past twenty years, but it has always been on a much smaller scale than our programs in Sudan, Afghanistan, East Africa, or other places overseas.

But when the COVID pandemic hit, the needs really ramped up. We went from serving 4,900 families in 2019 to more than 38,000 families in 2020, which added up to more than 160,000 individuals. While this is a reflection of people who need help, we have found that it is also an amazing opportunity to not only offer them groceries, but dignity as well.

Early on, our team came back from a food distribution and were very excited that they had served 120 families. I became lovingly blunt and transparent with them: "We're feeding more than 10,000 people in East Africa, and you're reacting like this about 120?" It wasn't the number that was the problem; it was this number in relation to the actual need. If there were only 120 to reach, then we could rejoice. But we knew that the problems of hunger around us were much bigger. I gently reminded them that we must not be guilty of asking God for too little.

To our team's credit, they rallied, and we began dreaming bigger—and God increased our reach to many more people in the St. Louis area, from 400 families a month to 4,000 families a month (at the time of this writing).

Along the way, we began feeling that God wanted us to give away more than just food—and that didn't mean preaching a sermon to everyone we served. Research shows that people react positively when they can help someone else. It literally releases chemicals and endorphins in their brains. As cities were burning and people were dying of disease, we knew that God wanted to give them more than food—He wanted to give them peace and a sense of purpose beyond their own life circumstances.

There can be a lack of dignity in huge food distributions, especially when you just throw food in people's trunks and they drive off. We wanted our interaction with the community to help foster systemic change, so we structured our concept around the idea of everyone being able to help others, even if they were the ones being helped. We tested the idea at one of our distribution events.

As usual, we gave people their groceries—a term much better than "food distribution," which can sound sterile and impersonal. But this time, we also put a very nice, well-written little label on their bag with a positive, affirming message—something that acknowledged their dignity, not just their need. Finally, before they pulled away, one of our staff or volunteers walked up to their window and gave them a few extra cans, asking them to give these cans to someone else they knew who needed groceries. We included them in the cycle of giving hope and dignity.

Some people literally broke down crying when we asked them to help us help others. The change in everyone's body language was a phenomenon that could be observed and studied for years. We took one of our core values—respect the dignity of all people—and invited everyone we served to join us in it.

Because we're all being served, we all need to also serve in some way—that is the key to the gospel and to basic human dignity.

THE EYE OF THE HURRICANE: LIFE IN THE CENTER OF GOD'S WILL

(A Glimpse from Susan's Perspective)

When Pat returned from his first trip to Russia, I knew things had changed. I had been watching the change ever since the Tuesday night he surrendered his life to God's grace. You've read our story now, and you know that our early years weren't pretty. They hurt so much that I felt no other option but to divorce him. This was one of the hardest things I ever did, but along the way, I became aware of what Pat has been telling you in every story you've just read: God was doing things in His own plan that were higher than the plans I could have made for myself or my family.

After Russia, Pat continued to go on a few missions trips here and there. This was our pattern for the first ten years of our second marriage, but I had no idea what was coming. When he came home from Sudan in 2000, I knew something significant had shifted in him yet again. When he couldn't speak for several weeks, I wanted to worry, but something inside offered me peace—and I chose to take it. Looking back, I know that God was guarding me in ways I will never be able to fully realize.

Pat's transition from chasing the next drink to chasing the epicenter of the next disaster was something incredible to witness. When he first mentioned going to Sudan, we were with another couple at dinner. I thought to myself, *Whoa, who is this guy?* But the peace was always there—a peace I never had throughout the six years that he drank away our marriage. Maybe we had already been through so much that God was using that memory of pain to keep me in a place of peace and trust. If God had brought us through all that, He had proven that He could bring us through anything. Pat was no longer my responsibility—he was serving Someone much more capable of not only keeping him safe, but also fulfilling his purpose.

As I like to say, being in the center of God's will is the safest place to be. It is like the eye of the hurricane—a place of inexplicable peace as two-hundred-mile-per-hour winds swirl around you in every direction. Staying in that center is the key to not getting blown away by fear. It is a choice, not a feeling. It is continuing to believe that God is in control, and thus resisting the temptation to keep trying to wrestle control from Him.

It's weird to have more peace when your husband is meeting with warlords than when he is drinking in the next room. That could only be a God thing. We had no cell phones in the early days, and even when we did, he was often in places so remote that there was no service. There were times when we couldn't speak for weeks at a time. Of course, I'm finally learning more about what was happening.

BEING IN THE CENTER OF GOD'S WILL IS THE SAFEST PLACE TO BE.

Most of it I already knew, but a few new details have emerged from the writing of this book. I didn't quite realize how many war zones Pat had been in. This does nothing but reinforce to me that God was with us, and that the peace He offered me was a priceless gift that continues to grow in value with each passing day. Pat always says that God gave him an adventurous heart, but He gave me a supernatural peace. He's right. In fact, I don't think our children ever truly realized that Pat was sometimes in danger—they were mostly out of high school during his trips to more dangerous situations, besides Afghanistan the first time. Other than that, we all heard the "missions trip" stories, things meant to gross them out over dinner, just for fun. We had peace.

In fact, when Pat went on that first Afghanistan trip, God spoke to my heart: "You have to hold Pat loosely. He belongs to me, and he is doing what I desire."

By 2003, the children had left the house, which meant that I could travel more with Pat. We flew into East Africa, and the moment we stepped off the plane, I not only saw the Pat Bradley that everyone in this whole other world got to see all the time, I also got to see the reasons God had placed these people and their situation upon His heart in the first place.

Our first thing to do on the trip was to attend a funeral for a mother who had died of starvation. My heart was broken over the devastating loss—and by the fact that it didn't have to be this way. Pat had once committed $100,000 that we didn't have to build that first therapeutic feeding center, but when I got there and saw the desperation for myself, I more deeply understood his willingness to say yes so freely—I got it deep down in my bones. They had absolutely nothing, which sounds foreign to Western ears, but it is literally true for them. If they were lucky, they might have a pot or a pan to cook what could be found, or a mat to sleep on.

How could we say no? How could we do nothing? I was always on board for all of it, but when I began going and being a part of it myself, it took on a whole new level of meaning and passion. Now, I've spent nearly two decades directly working to help those in need. It is a life I never could have envisioned— much better than any plan I would have written for myself.

Like Pat, I want to remind you that we're not superheroes or exceptional people. We were children who blew up our marriage before it could get off the ground. We were wrecked, but God graciously picked up the pieces and put us back to- gether. It's a simple story, not a grand one—the grandness is in God's part.

I was advised by my divorce attorney to go to Al-Anon. Later, he asked me if I had gone, and I told him I had only gone once. He must have known that I really needed it, because he told me something that made a huge difference in my life. He said, "Keep going until you want to go." This may seem like strange advice from a divorce attorney. We later found out that he was a recovering alcoholic himself. His wisdom gave me both permission and correction to get past my feelings. It's not that my feelings weren't important or valid; they just didn't have to completely dictate the course of my life. I need- ed Al-Anon, whether it felt great to go or not.

God was showing me that courage is from Him, so I could keep taking steps that hurt to take. I could keep making moves that were uncomfortable to make. I could overcome my fears and my feelings because He was empowering me to do so.

You can too. This isn't just about going on a trip or giving more money. This is about allowing God to pick you up and reassemble your wreckage, even if you look very polished and religious to everyone on the outside of your own soul. It isn't about doing good deeds or works to earn His approval of your life; it's about accepting His approval already paid for by Jesus and supplied by His grace so that your heart breaks for the same things that move Him to action. Then, you will find yourself doing the actions that Christ does for the people that He loves . . . because now, you will love them too. It is amazing what the Lord will do in your life if you are willing. And one thing we each had was a willing heart.

Someone Else's Shoes

I (Pat) really didn't want to write this book—who am I that someone would want to read my story? But God has been so good to me, and I am absolutely sure He will be the same for everyone who simply makes themselves available. I hope you have seen how God uses normal, broken people.

You've read some crazy stories, but I want to remind you that I lived with constant tension over who I was and whether I had any business being in these places or doing these things. I didn't just "get saved" and become some fearless *Braveheart* character. No blue warrior paint. No swords. No kilts.

I'm just a guy with the same insecurities as you—maybe more. I've done this long enough that I can say this plainly: I hate the way the devil has blinded our minds and our eyes to the reality that God really is there for us, rooting *for* us and not against us. We have developed the view of God that He is there to judge us—to find us innocent or guilty. We fail to realize that the best moment in life is when we realize we can't be innocent on our own, but that Jesus loved us so much that He already paid the price to redeem our guilt and declare us innocent. Not because we have to be good enough, but precisely because we are not capable of being good enough.

When we see God the wrong way, we live our lives as if we're not good enough or as if we don't have enough faith. We assume God is upset with us or that our status as disciples fluctuates with our good or bad days or deeds, so we can't trust Him or expect Him to answer our prayers. It's a weird pecking order of faith that we buy into, and we don't even realize that it's not based on God or His grace, but on our own self-centeredness. God didn't wait for us to get it right before He sent Jesus to die, and He's still not waiting on us to get it right in order to fight on our side. God already fights for you, and He wants to do it even more! When we doubt that He wants to help, we're literally stressing and hurting ourselves over a matter that's already been completely settled at the Cross.

I recently went back through many of my old journals from all of these incredible experiences you just read about, and there were some common themes. I always missed my wife, and I always begged God to let me hear His voice clearly. I often wrote from a place of scarcity, asking Him to show me what to do. It was an obsessive request from an insecure heart.

As I was begging God to let me hear Him, I was smuggling Bibles through airports in China to get them to underground churches. While I was asking Him to use me, I was spending months on end feeding the hungry in refugee camps and freeing young girls from sexual slavery. I wonder if God ever just shook His head with each of my requests and said, "Did you just see what I did in your life five minutes ago? What are you talking about? Of course I'm speaking to you and leading your life—can't you see that?"

This kind of thinking keeps us from trusting and taking action. Like Susan said, it's not just about doing more. It's about agreeing with God completely regarding what He says about you, your sin, your infinite value, and the infinite value of those in need around this world.

When you agree with Him, you stop worrying so much about your own childish insecurities that sound very religious and noble, but are truly worthless, wasteful energy suckers.

Sometimes people will ask me how I do it—whatever *it* is. They mean well, but I try to pivot their perspective to the better thing. I ask them to take five seconds and imagine what it must feel like to walk in the shoes of a young mother who is watching her baby die from starvation.

If I can show them her picture, that helps. If I can take them to where she lives, that is infinitely better. Why? Because it really all comes down to putting ourselves in others' shoes. Empathy leads to the right kind of action.

This is really the gospel, just in a way people don't usually think of it. The gospel is all about God seeing our suffering and refusing to do nothing about it, even though we caused it. His plan was to set aside His own heavenly state and put on humanity, with all our aches, pains, temptations, and fears. He walked in our shoes, and then He offered us the chance to walk in His grace for the rest of our lives on earth—and for an endless future. Many people's Christianity is lived from a subconsciously selfish perspective, not one that humbly examines the heart to continue journeying into grace, growth, and intimacy. I'm talking about the kind of introspection that always makes you feel worthless and unworthy so that you never step out and start taking action toward what God really cares about in this world.

It's easy to assume He's mad at you, or that you're the exception to what He cares about. This also makes you overlook what He cares about outside of you. You assume that though He can forgive all the sin in the world, yours is just a little worse—and you are just a little too unreachable. I've been there, and that's how I know that many Christians barely believe they are going to heaven, which makes them barely willing to fully live for Christ on earth.

Many will stand before God in heaven and realize just how much they were loved by Him—that He has prepared more for them for all eternity than their hearts and minds could even imagine. In that moment, they will rejoice for what's ahead, but weep for what's behind because they will realize all the wasted years they spent feeling like they were not enough.

They will finally hear the message that Jesus is already speaking to us today if we will only listen: "Look at all I have done for you and have for you to do! Why don't you just ask Me and trust that I'm answering abundantly?"

I sincerely believe that being a Christian should be the greatest adventure on the planet, but too many people sit in church bored to tears with their Christianity. It saddens me. They don't realize that their inaction is an action—that their lack of doing something is a vote for doing nothing. Doing nothing may feel neutral, but it supports and reinforces the status quo of whatever is happening. This is where the Church is most backwards.

BEING A CHRISTIAN SHOULD BE THE GREATEST ADVENTURE ON THE PLANET, BUT TOO MANY PEOPLE SIT IN CHURCH BORED TO TEARS WITH THEIR CHRISTIANITY.

We think remaining disengaged is doing no harm, when in fact, we are a part of the harm. If we know that girls are being sold into sexual slavery and we do nothing about it, then we may not openly support sex trafficking, but we are contributing to its flourishing.

Edmund Burke is thought to have said, "The only thing necessary for the triumph of evil is for good men to do nothing." The Bible agrees: "Remember, it is sin to know what you ought to do and then not do it" (James 4:17).

There are consequences for doing something, but there are also consequences for doing nothing. Again, this is not about earning your status before God, but rather fully believing the status already granted you through grace so that you are compelled and empowered to join in the works of God.

I was walking in the red-light district for the second or third time when I heard God say to my heart, "I gave this opportunity to someone else who did nothing with it. What are you going to do?" I don't know who it was, but I truly believe somebody else was called to go there before me. Obviously God's heart had been there the whole time. We weren't His first choice.

In the end, God will accomplish all His purposes in this world—and He can do it with or without us. For now, He has chosen to make us a big part of the execution of His will on this planet. He says this plainly in Scripture over and over again when we are called the body and He is called the head.

We are supposed to be inseparably connected, sharing the same thoughts and actions because we are one with Him and one another.

What do you think Jesus thinks about poverty and trafficking? What do you think He is doing to address them? Whatever those thoughts and actions are, they are now supposed to be ours as well. Sitting in the pews and calling it Christianity has ramifications. It's not nothing; it's something we were never meant to do.

But what would you do differently if you knew God was with you and that ultimately, you could not fail?

In the next minute, when you put this book on your shelf or coffee table, I pray that you will hear Jesus affectionately speaking your name as He did mine. I pray that you will remember the people in these stories not because of me, but because God sent me to help them because He loves us all so immensely. I pray that you will realize that I did many things wrong, but I did keep saying yes—and after that, all I did was show up. He did the rest—that is, He wrote the parts of the stories that make them worth telling.

That's all you have to do too—just keeping saying yes.

ACKNOWLEDGMENTS

First of all, I never set out to write a book, so I'm grateful to the Lord for giving me a story to tell. God has led me in so many unlikely adventures with so many wonderful people over the years—and now, I am in awe that He has led me to share on this level about their incredible stories of His eternal faithfulness.

To my wife, Susan, you have been my constant companion in every season, even the ones that weren't so easy. You never faltered. Thank you for seeing me through the eyes of Jesus and staying by my side through this crazy, amazing life we've lived together. Sue, I love you more than you will ever know. To my children, Rebecca and Shawn, being your dad and the grandchildren's "Papa" has been one of the greatest joys of my life. Many thanks to Rebecca and Shawn for all the love, support and sacrifices you have provided the past 30 plus years. You have been with us every step of this journey and we are so proud of both of you and you're your supportive spouses Chris and Cory. Thank you for making room in our lives for so many others around the world who need the kind of love you continue to show me.

To my friend and agent, Wayne Hastings, and to my collaborative writer, John Driver, thank you for dreaming with me and pushing me to make this book a reality, even when I didn't always enjoy the idea of doing it. In the end, I know many will be enriched in the same way these stories have enriched my life. To David Henriksen, John Crowe, Kobus Johnson, and the entire editorial, design, and marketing team at iDisciple, thank you for believing in this message and for being enthusiastic and diligent partners in seeing it become what we now hold in our hands.

To our incomparable staff and board at Crisis Aid, Warrine Bazow, Mike Lemp, Dr Henok and Betty Ghebrehiwot, Dane Welch, Caroli Young, Jerry Fitzgerald, Chris Igo, James Fillingame, and so many more, we remain eternally grateful to God every day for your hearts to feed the hungry, rescue the enslaved, heal the broken, and love the forgotten ones living at the epicenter of disaster. To all the others, too numerous to mention, who pray and partner with us in this journey, may these words encourage and uplift us all to continue to see and move towards those in need, just as God has seen us and continues to move in our direction for our good.

Finally, to everyone we have written about in this book, along with your families and friends, we pray that your stories have been honored well in a way that will lift up Jesus and draw others to refuse to do nothing.

ABOUT THE AUTHOR

In September of 2000, Pat Bradley watched out a back car window as a huddled group of fleeing survivors became smaller and smaller behind him. Their village had faced a murderous nighttime attack, a tragically familiar story amid the genocide occurring in South Sudan. In this moment, Pat realized that for the rest of his life, "doing nothing" was no longer an option. But he was just a former alcoholic and divorcee who worked in advertising—what could he possibly do?

Pat's helplessness was the impetus of a divine plan to propel him into action in ways he never imagined—by a strength far beyond his own. By linking arms with incredible partners around the globe—heroes most people have never heard of, they began to help displaced, maltreated, forgotten individuals in areas and situations mostly unknown and unseen by the world at large . What began with a return to Sudan to provide single bags of rice to people in need eventually led to the establishment of Crisis Aid, an international organization that specializes in showing up in "no-go zones" where starvation, disease, and danger are a part of everyday life. After working in eleven different countries, today Crisis Aid concentrates its efforts in East Africa and the United States.

Together with its partners, Crisis Aid has provided more than twenty million pounds of food, served over three million adults and malnourished children, and have helped bring hope and rescue to thousands of victims of sex trafficking, the youngest being four years old. Crisis Aid is committed to "helping the helpless" with relief efforts locally and globally, equipping those who are beyond the crisis to take responsibility by providing programs that train, inspire, and move those in extreme need to independent, self-sustaining living.

But for Pat Bradley, it's still about refusing to do nothing, just as God did for him—freeing him from alcohol addiction, restoring his marriage, and writing the unlikely adventure of a lifetime on every page of his normal life. Pat lives in St. Louis with Susan, his wife of more than forty years. They have two adult children and 6 grandchildren.

ABOUT THE
COLLABORATOR

John Driver, M.S. is an award-winning writer and collaborator of more than twenty-eight books. He has been featured on Good Morning America (GMA3), Sirius XM Radio, and numerous other media outlets and podcasts. A former teacher with a History degree from the University of Tennessee, he lives near Nashville with his wife and daughter. He serves as the executive and teaching pastor at The Church at Pleasant Grove and hosts the weekly podcast Talk About That.